FINGERPRINTS

FINGERPRINTS

ANALYSIS AND UNDERSTANDING THE SCIENCE

MARK R. HAWTHORNE
SHARON L. PLOTKIN
BRACEY-ANN DOUGLAS

CRC Press
Taylor & Francis Group
Boca Raton London New York

CRC Press is an imprint of the
Taylor & Francis Group, an **informa** business

Second edition published 2021
by CRC Press
6000 Broken Sound Parkway NW, Suite 300, Boca Raton, FL 33487-2742

and by CRC Press
2 Park Square, Milton Park, Abingdon, Oxon, OX14 4RN

© 2021 Taylor & Francis Group, LLC

First edition published by CRC Press 2009

CRC Press is an imprint of Taylor & Francis Group, LLC

Reasonable efforts have been made to publish reliable data and information, but the author and publisher cannot assume responsibility for the validity of all materials or the consequences of their use. The authors and publishers have attempted to trace the copyright holders of all material reproduced in this publication and apologize to copyright holders if permission to publish in this form has not been obtained. If any copyright material has not been acknowledged please write and let us know so we may rectify in any future reprint.

Except as permitted under U.S. Copyright Law, no part of this book may be reprinted, reproduced, transmitted, or utilized in any form by any electronic, mechanical, or other means, now known or hereafter invented, including photocopying, microfilming, and recording, or in any information storage or retrieval system, without written permission from the publishers.

For permission to photocopy or use material electronically from this work, access www.copyright.com or contact the Copyright Clearance Center, Inc. (CCC), 222 Rosewood Drive, Danvers, MA 01923, 978-750-8400. For works that are not available on CCC please contact mpkbookspermissions@tandf.co.uk

Trademark notice: Product or corporate names may be trademarks or registered trademarks and are used only for identification and explanation without intent to infringe.

Library of Congress Cataloging-in-Publication Data

ISBN: 978-0-367-47950-3 (hbk)
ISBN: 978-0-367-47951-0 (pbk)
ISBN: 978-1-003-03736-1 (ebk)

Typeset in Minion
by MPS Limited, Dehradun

Contents

Preface ix
Acknowledgments xi
About the Authors xiii

Part I: Fingerprint Analysis

1 The History of Fingerprints 3

Outline of the History of Fingerprints 4
    Early Cases Resulting in the Acceptance of Fingerprints 9
Early Nonsystematic Methods of Identification 11
Chapter 1 Study Questions 13

2 Systematic Methods of Identification 15

Bertillonage 16
Fingerprints 20
    Definitions Associated with Fingerprints 20
    Fingerprint Patterns and Ridge Characteristics 24
    More Fingerprint Definitions 25
Chapter 2 Study Questions 27

3 Fingerprint Pattern Types and Associated Terminology 29

Loop Pattern 29
Loop Ridge Counting 34
Radial and Ulnar Loops 35
Other Issues Pertaining to Loops 36
Plain Arch and Tented Arch Patterns 39
    The Plain Arch 39
    The Tented Arch 39
The Whorl Pattern 41
    Plain Whorl 43
    Central Pocket Loop Whorl 44
    Double Loop Whorl 50

Accidental Whorl 52
Ridge Tracing and Counting Whorl Patterns 54
The Palm Print 55
Chapter 3 Study Questions 57

4 Introduction to Classification Systems 59

Henry with FBI Extension 59
Ridge Count Conversion 66
Conversion Chart for Ridge Counts 66
Referencing 70
Filing Sequence 71
NCIC Classification System 72
IAFIS 73
Other Fingerprint Systems (Manual Methods or Systems) 74
Chapter 4 Study Questions 75

Part II: Development, Identification, and Presentation of Fingerprints

5 Known/Direct/Inked Fingerprints: Processing Technique for Unknown/Latent Fingerprints 79

Known Fingerprints 79
Manual Method 79
Live Scan 88
Unknown Fingerprints (Commonly Referred to as Latent Prints) ... 89
Conditions Affecting Latent Prints 90
The Crime Scene Search and Fingerprint Development 91
Fingerprint Development Techniques 93
    Powder Techniques 94
    Chemical Techniques 104
    Ardrox Dye Stain—Aqueous Premix 120
    Basic Yellow 40 Dye Stain 120
Fingerprint Comparison and Identification 131
Chapter 5 Study Questions 143

6 Court Preparation and Presentation 145

Preparation of the Exhibit 145
Courtroom Etiquette 147
Qualifying the Expert Witness 147

Contents

Courtroom Testimony 148
Presentation of the Exhibit 149
The historic case that allowed fingerprint evidence in the courtroom ... 149
Review 149
Challenges to the Science of Fingerprints 151
Federal Rules of Evidence Rule 702 152
Chapter 6 Study Questions 153

Appendix A 155

Appendix B 159

Appendix C 163

Bibliography 167

Glossary 169

Index 173

Preface

Friction skin and fingerprints have long been considered the parts of the anatomy that serve a specific purpose. Since the beginning of mankind, observations of friction skin on the inner hands and bottoms of the feet have given observers something to think about as these particular areas have an appearance significantly different from other parts of the skin.

Since the beginning, the purpose of friction skin has been explored. As time evolved and the degree of sophistication and education increased, the purpose and the uses of friction skin were slowly discovered by those early pioneers who took it upon themselves to research its varied uses. It soon became quite evident that friction skin had more uses than simply utilitarian. As the uniqueness of the composition of friction skin was discovered, it was determined and could be used to identify individuals. The recognition of the different uses of friction skin, and specifically fingerprints, did not occur in a vacuum or overnight. It has only been within the past three to four hundred years, a time in which technology has allowed such research, that the true marvel uses of friction skin, and specifically fingerprints, have come to the forefront. Since that time, many issues surrounding fingerprints and footprints have become part of the evolution of fingerprint science. Some would argue that the study of fingerprints is not truly a science, but strictly an art.

The study of fingerprints is akin to any other science. There are sets of assumptions that must be proved or disproved. As with other sciences, the science of fingerprint study, has grown by leaps and bounds over the past one hundred years. Various techniques and research that have been undertaken serve only to strengthen the position of the science. However, we must ask ourselves what must be done to maintain the integrity of the science of fingerprints? What is needed is an educational process, guidelines and protocols to train practitioners, both advocates and critics alike, in the strengths and weaknesses of fingerprints as a form of identification, whether in the field or in the courtroom, and recognition to those who work in the field of latent processing of fingerprints with a need for a basic understanding of the applications.

The National Academy of Sciences (NAS) report in 2009 was established to guarantee that continued improvements will support law enforcement officials in the work responsibilities during investigations to identify offenders with higher reliability. This report examines forensic disciplines including friction ridge analysis. Historically, friction ridge analysis served as a valuable tool to identify the guilty and exclude the innocent. Due to the amount of detail presented in friction ridges, it appears that a vigilant comparison of two impressions can accurately discern whether they have a common source. Despite the limited information regarding the accuracy and reliability of friction ridge analyses, claims that these analyses have zero error rates are not scientifically plausible.

Continued improvements in forensic science practices should reduce the incidence of wrongful convictions, which decreases the risk that true offenders continue to commit crimes while innocent persons unfortunately serve time. The quality of forensic practice in most disciplines differs greatly because of the lack of adequate training and continuing education, rigorous mandatory certification and accreditation programs, observance to rigorous performance standards, and oversight. These shortfalls create a continuing and serious threat to the quality and credibility of forensic science practice. Therefore, it is incumbent upon all law enforcement personnel whether it is crime scene technicians, latent examiners, or lab personnel that we adhere to rigorous standards and protocols in effective investigations and successful outcomes (Strengthening Forensic Science in the United States: A Path Forward, National Academy of Sciences, 2009).

It is the hope of these authors that this publication will provide an introduction to understanding the concepts associated with friction skin, specifically fingerprints and to the development process.

Many publications that have been produced recently are of an advanced nature topically. The intent of this publication is to provide the basics in understanding the principles, applications, techniques, and uses of fingerprints. One cannot be expected to solve any complex equation without first obtaining basic formulas with which to work. The science of fingerprints is not different. While complex, at its heart, the simplicity of the science mandates its usefulness.

Acknowledgments

There are many people that I want to acknowledge for their contributions either directly or indirectly in the development of a career, which in turn has made it possible for me to write this book. I want to thank those individuals by specifically naming them. If I have overlooked anyone who feels they have contributed, I apologize. There is no way I can truly recognize all those who have had an impact on my professional development.

I want to begin by thanking the person most instrumental in providing the opportunity for me to enter into the field of forensic identification. That person is Ken Moses. Thank you for all of your encouragement and support by requesting me to be transferred into the Crime Scene Investigation Unit.

As my career progressed, I met George and Donna Jewett who have lent support and fellowship for me to prosper. By way of instruction, I want to thank Bill Bray, Joe Rynerson, Ron Smith, Pat Wertheim, Bruce Wiley, and the plethora of others who have assisted me in developing my professional skills and abilities. I would also like to make a special acknowledgment of Robert Prouty who acted as a mentor to me in my early years within the forensic discipline. Many of my professional colleagues whom I would like to thank hail from a variety of agencies. Those individuals are: Norm and Dee Bettencourt, Maggie Black, Diana Castro, Bill Corson, Robert Dagitz, Charles Hoenisch, Jim Kinavey, Martin Kilgariff, Dan and Larry Lawson, former chief of police of San Francisco, Thomas Murphy, Ann Punter, Al Trigueiro, and Joe Zamani. I have been truly blessed to have found a career and the opportunity to pass along the information I have developed to others who are the future of the Forensic Community.

And of course, no true acknowledgment would be complete without including family who have been so supportive over the many years of my pursuit of the field and professional career.

—**Mark Hawthorne (From the First Edition)**

In one's life only a handful of people pass through that significantly change the path our lives will take, and it is because of them that I am who I am today.

I am truly thankful for so many people in my life, but I begin by saying that without the support from my husband Richard and my beautiful family, Bonnie, Ally, Andi, and David that this opportunity could not have been possible. Thank you for sacrificing so many moments we could have been together in recognizing the importance of sharing knowledge with others.

Thank you to Mark, our editor, for the faith in us to further create a rich textbook that you see in front of you.

Lastly, thank you to Madai Batista, Johan Bravo, Iana Azoy, and the people who believed in me so that I could share my passion for this work. I too learned from you and you complete me.

—**Sharon L. Plotkin**

The journey of life may lead one down many paths, but the experiences gain throughout that time are well worthwhile. A lesson is learned from every incident, whether good or bad. Therefore, I welcome all adversity and use it to persevere in life.

All members of my family have been supportive throughout the process, and I am grateful to have them. I want to truly thank Sharon Plotkin, because without her pouring knowledge into me, I would have not afforded this opportunity and many others.

Thank you, Mark for allowing me to be a part of another great experience in life. My very first work to be published.

—**Bracey-Ann Douglas**

About the Authors

Mark R. Hawthorne, now retired, was previously a Professor and faculty member at the City College of San Francisco, where he started teaching in 1985 in the Administration of Justice programs and had also served as the coordinator of the forensic science program in criminal justice. In addition, he was an instructor at Skyline College in San Bruno, California among other universities. He holds an associate of arts, bachelor of arts, and master's degrees. He has taken more than one thousand hours of technical training regarding fingerprints, physical evidence, and crime scene processing. He was also previously the lead instructor in physical evidence and crime scenes at the San Francisco Police Regional Training Academy.

Hawthorne is a retired member of the San Francisco Police Department after serving with distinction for twenty-nine years, the last twenty-three years as a crime scene investigator. During his career, Hawthorne has processed more than 3,000 crime scenes, processed thousands of pieces of evidence, and testified as an expert witness numerous times in California state courts as well as U.S. district courts. He has conducted thousands of fingerprint comparisons and has made in excess of 3,000 identifications. Hawthorne has been an I.A.I. Certified Latent Print Examiner as well as a Certified Senior Crime Scene Analyst. He has also been recognized as a subject matter expert by the State of California Commission on Peace Officer Standards and Training in subject matter of physical evidence and crime scenes.

In addition to solely authoring the first edition of this book, Hawthorne has made numerous presentations to various forensic organizations and meetings, and is a published author (*First Unit Responder: A Guide for the Physical Evidence Collection for Patrol Officers*). He has also mentored and assisted countless students to achieve the goal in the field of Forensic Science.

Hawthorne lives in San Francisco with his wife and is the father of two children.

Sharon L. Plotkin obtained a master's of science degree in Criminal Justice with a minor in Psychology from Florida International University. She also obtained her bachelor of science degree in Social Work from Florida

International University and an associate of arts degree in Psychology from Broward Community College.

Plotkin received her certification through the International Association for Identification in 2006 and has been doing crime scene work for almost twenty years. She has handled thousands of cases ranging from burglaries to homicides and suspicious death cases.

Plotkin has a passion for teaching and loves the opportunity to excite students in wanting to embark on a career in law enforcement. She has been teaching at the college level for almost 13 years. She is full-time faculty at the largest school in the nation that currently has 165,000 students enrolled, teaching in the crime scene technology degree program.

Plotkin has received specialized training in various fields of crime scene investigations, including bloodstain reconstruction, photography, crime scene reconstruction, fingerprinting, and shoe wear casting. She has had the opportunity to be involved in casework with Dr. Henry Lee, assisting in crime scene reconstruction. Some of her cases have appeared on *Court TV*. She is also a member of DMORT (Disaster Mortuary Operational Response Team).

Plotkin taught courses for Dr. Henry Lee as well as throughout the United States. She has been a lecturer at several mystery writers' conferences as well as all over the country assisting them in "keeping it real."

Plotkin has five fabulous daughters and a grandson Noah. She loves approaching every classroom and crime scene as a new adventure and looks at each one from a new perspective. She loves not knowing what is waiting for her each day. She also feels that training students and law enforcement are her greatest inspiration.

Bracey-Ann Douglas holds a master's of science degree in Management with a Concentration in Criminal Justice Administration from St. Thomas University, a bachelor of applied science in Public Safety Management with Concentration in Crime Scene Investigations from Miami Dade College and an associate in arts in Criminal Justice from Miami Dade College.

Douglas has been in the criminal justice field for the past ten years, where she obtained numerous trainings in the field of fingerprints and crime scene. She was trained at the Federal Bureau of Investigations Headquarters in Clarksburg, West Virginia at the Criminal Justice Information System Section on fingerprint identification, comparison, and courtroom testimony.

Douglas is currently a Police Officer in the Miami-Dade County Police Department, Northside District, where she handles numerous homicide cases. She worked previously in the Miami-Dade County Corrections and Rehabilitation Department in the Fingerprint Section as a Fingerprint

Analyst, where she analyzed, classified, and compared fingerprints for courtroom purposes.

Prior to that, she was a Crime Scene Technician with the City of North Miami Police Department's Crime Scene Unit. She is currently an Adjunct Faculty Professor in the Miami Dade College's North Campus School of Justice providing classroom instruction, curriculum development, and supervisor for students' field experience and internships. She enjoys the classroom environment and shares the everyday real-life experiences with her students.

Part I

Fingerprint Analysis

The History of Fingerprints 1

Fingerprints have been a constant since the birth of mankind. Over several thousand years, man has been in existence, fingerprints have not changed. Evolution has simply necessitated the analysis and understanding of the skin we possess on our hands and feet. What was once viewed simply as a covering for our skeletal/musculature mass, with distinct characteristics and configuration, we now know has a specific definition and application. As with all things in nature, we possess uniqueness within each of us. This uniqueness is not limited to mankind, but to all primates as well, which was first observed and documented by Johannes (John) Evangelista Purkinje in 1823. Prior to that time, there are documented instances where finger and palm prints were observed but no formal study or analysis was undertaken. The uniqueness of the impressions was captured, but the specificity as to the individualization was not pursued. There are documented instances within various prehistoric sites, as well as other discoveries throughout the world, that indicate fingerprints were somehow used as a method of identity most probably for psychological or superstitious purposes. There has been no supporting documentation of a formula that may have been used with those findings. Assumptions, simple or complex, must be utilized in an attempt to explain the presence of the fingerprints.

It has been well documented that fingerprints have been discovered on mummies in Egypt as well as other artifacts from Mesopotamia and in cave drawings in Nova Scotia. Further examples of the use of fingerprints can be found in Chinese documents from the Tang dynasty, which allude to fingerprints impressed on business contracts. Prehistoric carvings of fingerprints have been noted in France, and finger imprints discovered on broken pottery in Palestine as well. One can see that in one form or another, fingerprints or the fascination with fingerprints is nothing new. One is looking at thousands of years of viewing, in one fashion or another, the fingerprints we all possess. Why then today do we have such a command of fingerprints? What factor(s) can be cited that instigated, in earnest, the research that has laid the foundation for interpretation and analysis of fingerprints? The answer to those questions is multifaceted. However, I believe the main focal point to the equation may be said to coincide with the study of other aspects of the human anatomy, science, and medicine. These disciplines, by their very nature, necessitate that a meticulous methodology is utilized and documented. Theories must be postulated and proved or disproved. With the earliest developments of fingerprint study, practitioners became immersed in the research. As the field became more deeply understood, and the practices more widespread, those practitioners who took up the research and training rose to the level of scientists. The science of fingerprints began with professionals of the day and has expanded to the much more technical application we now know. Does the more technical nature of fingerprint analysis negate the science? Absolutely not. The technical applications serve only to enhance the knowledge that has been established throughout more than four hundred years of research, all of which have contributed to the science. Principles and theories that have been well established will not be diminished. But as with all scientific practices, we must remain vigilant and open to new ideas and theories that may have application to the science of fingerprints.

A brief history of the development of the science and of those who have contributed to this development is outlined. This outline is not all-inclusive but rather foundational. As new research is undertaken and discoveries are made, modification of the outline will be needed. What follows is an overview of the timeline of significant developments, as well as individuals and their contributions to the science.

Outline of the History of Fingerprints

> **7000 BC Jericho:** Neolithic bricks from the ancient city were discovered to contain thumbprints of bricklayers. This information was reported in a modern publication in *Archaeology of the Holy Land*, a book researched and written by Dame K. Kenyon.
>
> **3000 BC Northwest Europe at New Grange, Republic of Ireland, and Brittany, France:** Artifacts have been found in these locations to contain carvings of fingerprints. Artifacts such as the inner burial chamber passages and tombs possess the images of fingerprint ridges. Although some say that the prints were coincidentally placed on the artifacts by the artisans, the Stockis theory states that the placement of prints was intentional.
>
> **1955–1913 BC Babylon** (Hammurabi): It is said that fingerprints were used to seal contracts.

AD 600–700 Ancient China: Kia Kung-Yen, a Chinese historian of the Tang period, mentions fingerprints being used to seal contracts and legal documents. *Yung-Hwui*, a law book, specified that in order to divorce a husband must present a document giving the reasons for the action. All letters must be in his handwriting, but if unable to write, he must sign with his fingerprints. It is also said that sales of children were to be sealed with their sole and handprints.

From the history, we can see that there was curiosity and possibly a purposeful focus on fingerprints, but the modern era of the development of fingerprints and the research exacted its place in history. The following outlines those pioneers in the field of fingerprints, and their contributions, whether they were of limited or enormous value.

1684 Dr. Nehemiah Grew, a fellow of the Royal College of Physicians and a plant morphologist, commented on the ridge formations of the fingers. He is seen as the first pioneer to study and describes sweat pores, epidermal ridges and furrows, and their various arrangements on both the hands and feet. His works also included publications with accurate drawings. Dr. Grew died in 1712.

1686 Marcello Malpighi, a professor of anatomy at the University of Bologna, Italy, and a contemporary of Grew, took up his own studies and with the aid of a new device, the microscope, conducted his own research. He wrote many treatises on the palmar surfaces. His papers were primarily focused on function, form, and structure of the friction skin as a tactile organ and its use in the enhancement of traction for walking and grasping. He is credited with noting diverse figures on the palmar surfaces which appeared to be loops and spirals. For his research, and in recognition of his contributions, a layer of skin was named in his honor, the Malpighian layer, which is located on the stratum mucosum or the lower (inner) portion of the epidermal layer of skin. Malpighi failed to pursue further research in this area, and the developments he pioneered fell silent for more than one hundred years.

1788 J.C.A. Mayer, a German scientist, became the first to expound on the theory that the arrangement of skin ridges is never duplicated in two individuals. "Although the arrangements of skin ridges are never duplicated in two persons, nevertheless the similarities are closer among some individuals. In others the differences are marked, yet in spite of their peculiarities of arrangement all have a certain likeness."

1823 Johannes Purkinje (or John Evangelist Purkinje or Jonnes Evangelista Purkinje), a Prussian, published a thesis in which he described friction ridge patterns and classified the fingerprints, dividing them into nine categories and laying down the rules for their interpretation. This was the first time prints were classified into patterns. Four basic patterns emerged: arch, tent, loop, and whorl.

1858 Sir William Herschel, British chief administrative officer of the Hooghly District, Bengal, India, is credited with the first known official use of fingerprints on a large scale. He required natives to affix their fingerprints as well as signatures to contracts. In 1877, Herschel submitted a request to the Home Office to use fingerprints extensively throughout India. Although his request was denied, Herschel implemented the first wide-scale use of fingerprints throughout his province in India. He failed, however, to establish an effective fingerprint classification system. Herschel also published an article in 1880 after reading articles by Dr. H. Faulds which led to allegations of plagiarism.

1880 Dr. Henry Faulds, a Scottish medical missionary who spent a year in India, later traveled to Japan and arrived in March of 1874. He set up a hospital in Tsuki, Tokyo. He suggested the use of fingerprints not only for identification, but also for criminal investigation and is credited with making the earliest known identification from a crime scene. He claimed two cases, one to convict and one to exonerate. It is also said that Faulds recommended the use of printer's ink for known fingerprint recording. Printer's ink is still used today to record many fingerprints.

1882 Gilbert Thompson, of the U.S. Geological Survey, recorded his own prints to prevent their forgery on commissary orders. This was the first such known use of fingerprints in the United States.

1882 Alphonse Bertillon devised anthropometry (also known as Bertillonage) while a clerk in the Paris Police Identification Bureau. Later named head of Sûreté Nationale, his system of identification was adopted throughout France. Bertillon claimed one of the first identifications using his system in February 20, 1883. A man named Martin was attempting to pass himself off as Dupont. Bertillon's system of body measurements was supplemented by the presence of fingerprints registered on the rear of his anthropometry cards, which are alleged to have led to more identifications than his system of anthropometry.

1883 Mark Twain: In his book *Life on the Mississippi*, Twain refers to the identification of a murderer by his thumbprint. Ten years later in another book, *Pudd'nhead Wilson*, a theme centered on a fingerprint identification demonstrated during a court trial in which the infallibility of fingerprint identification was espoused. What is remarkable about this notation is its date and Twain's knowledge of fingerprints.

1891 Juan Vucetich (Dr. Ivan Vucetich) was employed as a statistician with the Central Police Department, La Plata, Argentina. He was ordered to set up the Bertillonage system. He read an article by pioneer Francis Galton, formulated his own identification system, and implemented the system in September 1891. His system became known as "Vucetichissimo." Subsequently, he was ordered to discard his system and revert back to Bertillonage. Fortunately in 1896, before the revision could take place, Argentina abandoned Bertillonage and Vucetichissimo was retained. Vucetich's system is still used in South America. Vucetich claimed to make one of the first criminal identifications in 1892 in La Plata, Argentina.

1892 Sir Francis Galton, a British anthropologist and cousin of Darwin, began observations that led to the publication of "Finger Prints." This publication was the first on fingerprints. In it, Galton made the statement that fingerprints remain unchanged for life and they are permanent. He also devised the first scientific method of classifying fingerprint patterns into arches, loops, and whorls. Galton also pointed out ridge characteristics and described a method for taking prints. In recognition of the contributions by Galton, ridge characteristics were named in his honor and today are known as "Galton" details.

1893 Troup Committee (England) investigated fingerprinting and officially adopted it as a supplementary system of identification in 1894. In 1901, the "Belper Commission," recommended the use of the Henry Classification System, which was introduced at Scotland Yard.

1901 Sir Edward Henry made the official introduction of and the use of fingerprints for criminal identification at Scotland Yard. Henry, Herschel's successor in India, used fingerprints on payrolls. He also wrote "Classification and Uses of Fingerprints," published in England in 1901. Henry was appointed assistant commissioner of Scotland Yard in 1901 and is credited with developing and instituting a manual fingerprint system used worldwide today. However, this feat was not accomplished without controversy. It is said that Henry covertly gave his name to the classification system worked out by his Indian employees Khan Bahadur Azizul Haque and Rai Bahadur Hem Chandra

Bose. It was reasoned that as the English official in charge, he supported and encouraged his staff and should be ultimately responsible for the system. The action taken by Henry has been cause of resentment by some.

1902 Dr. Henry P. De Forest: Dr. De Forest is responsible for the first large-scale documented instance of fingerprints being used as a systematic method of identification in the United States. Dr. De Forest installed the system to prevent cheating by applicants for the New York Civil Service Commission. The system was installed in December 1902.

1903 Captain James Parke: The New York State prison system installed the first systematic use of fingerprints in the United States for use in identification of criminals. The system was officially adopted in June 1903.

1904 Ft. Leavenworth, Kansas/St. Louis, Missouri: Both the U.S. Penitentiary at Ft. Leavenworth and the St. Louis police department established fingerprint bureaus.

1904 Sgt. John K. Ferrier accompanied the Crown jewels to the St. Louis World's fair where he also instructed American police in the Henry system. Subsequently, a young woman named Mary Holland, who was a student learning the Henry system, went throughout the United States teaching the Henry system to many law enforcement agencies. This is a significant development, as the presence of women in law enforcement during this period was an unusual occurrence. Mary Holland is said to have been one of the strongest proponents of the Henry system and single-handedly was responsible for the accelerated acceptance of the Henry system throughout the United States.

1905 U.S. Army: Adoption of a fingerprint system began and was completed in 1906. This marks the first official use by the military in the United States. Over the next three years, the Navy and Marines would also develop and implement their own fingerprint systems.

1924 Federal Bureau of Investigation (FBI): The identification division was developed and instituted in 1924 with the files drawn from the records at Ft. Leavenworth, as was the National Bureau of Criminal Identification, which consisted of many submissions by police departments throughout the country to the FBI.

1933 FBI: The FBI established a latent fingerprint section for making technical examinations of latent prints or of inked prints on an individual basis. A civil identification section was also established that same year.

1974 Golden Anniversary of the FBI Identification Division: This is the world's largest repository of fingerprints.

1980 Development of various automated fingerprint identification systems (AFISs): Throughout the world, technology met fingerprints, and various types of "AFIS" systems began making their appearance with various law enforcement agencies. With the advent of AFISs, the process of filing and searching of fingerprints was considerably shortened. What used to take months now was completed in minutes. The manual method of identification, classification, filing, and searching was giving way to a more accelerated method of identification.

2000 and Beyond: The speed and accuracy of the various AFISs being used worldwide would only increase. As employees became more familiar with the operating systems, the ability to solve crimes and make identifications became astounding. The issue of disparate operating systems posed significant issues in that the various systems could not interface due to proprietary issues. The FBI, in establishing a super-AFIS, mandated that the new Integrated AFIS (IAFIS) be capable of interfacing with all current AFISs. That mandate has been a reality for several years.

Early Cases Resulting in the Acceptance of Fingerprints

1893 Argentina, June 19: In the small town of Necochea, two small children of young Francisca Rojas were murdered. Mrs. Rojas told the local police that she suspected a man named Velasquez who worked at a nearby ranch. Velasquez had threatened to kill the children when Mrs. Rojas, a widow, refused to marry him. Mrs. Rojas further stated that when she came home from work, Velasquez had run from her hut and passed her without a word. In the bedroom, she found her children dead. Velasquez was arrested and denied the murders. The police chief had him beaten then bound and laid beside the corpses for a night. After a full week of brutal interrogation, he still denied the crime. It was learned that Francisca had a young lover who had said that he would marry her only if she did not have the children. The suspicions of the police focused on the mother. Police Inspector Alvarez was sent from La Plata to investigate the matter. He established that Velasquez and Mrs. Rojas's lover had been elsewhere at the time of the murder. In searching the scene of the crime, he observed bloody fingerprints on the door of the hut. He cut out two pieces of the door bearing the prints and, along with the known fingerprints of Mrs. Rojas and Velasques, sent them to the La Plata Central Identification Bureau and Juan Vucetich. The latent prints were identified as those of the mother and, when faced with this evidence, she confessed.

1914 Canada: The first conviction in Canada based on fingerprint evidence took place. Peter Caracatch and Gregory Parachique broke into the CPR station in Petawawa, Ontario. Their fingerprints, left at the point of entry, were subsequently used to convict the offenders.

1902 France: Joseph Reibel was found murdered in an apartment in Paris. In the drawing room, a glass door of a cabinet had been broken and on a portion of the remaining glass, several latent fingerprints were discovered. The investigation of the traces was assigned to Alphonse Bertillon who compared the latent prints with his anthropometric cards on which finger impressions were also recorded. Bertillon's report read in part, "As this search was conducted with the greatest care it led to the discovery of a record card concerning one Henri Leon Scheffer, age 26, measured last March 9 as he was charged with theft and swindle, and whose fingerprints match remarkably those discovered at the crime scene." As a result of this report, Scheffer's photograph was recognized by several eyewitnesses and the culprit was eventually arrested in Marseille. He was brought to Paris where he was convicted in 1903.

1897 India: The manager of a tea garden in Bengal was found murdered in his bedroom. The room was in great disarray and the safe rifled. Two brown smudges of fingerprints were found on a Bengali almanac. Upon examination at the Central Office in Calcutta, Sir Edward Henry found the prints to be those of Kangali Charan whose thumbprint had been recorded because of a prior theft conviction. Charan was now indicted for murder and theft at the Court of Session at Jalpaiguiri. Confronted with the novel type of evidence consisting of fingerprints only, and in the face of the defendant's not-guilty plea, the court seemed sufficiently convinced of the worth of fingerprints to find Charan guilty of the theft charge, yet not quite willing to accept the evidence to substantiate a capital charge. The accused, Charan, was acquitted of murder.

1911 United States: Chicago police arrested a man named Thomas Jennings for murder. Jennings had murdered a man when he had been caught attacking the man's daughter. The evidence against Jennings was slim except for fingerprint evidence. The prosecution wanted to ensure the fingerprint evidence would be admitted before the Illinois Supreme Court, which had not previously ruled on the issue. To strengthen its case, the prosecution called several recognized fingerprint experts as witnesses. Among the expert witnesses was Mary E. Holland of Holland Detective Agency. As a result, Jennings was convicted and sentenced to hang on December 22, 1911.

The aforementioned cases serve to illustrate, as with any new technology, that test cases must establish the viability of evidence. Today we realize, without question, that fingerprints are one of the most damaging types of evidence that can be presented due to the individuality that can be established. In other words, fingerprints can be individualized to one source to the exclusion of all others.

There are certainly documented instances of other methods of identification being developed and implemented for such purposes as criminal or civil identification long before the systematic method of identifying and using fingerprints become widely used. To better understand the methodology of fingerprint science, its specificity, and its importance, a short examination of early methods of identification should be explored. Although widely used for many hundreds of years, how effective were early forms of identification? Was there the ability to authenticate a method of identification? Was that method of identification subject to peer review? Could the results be replicated? We have collectively learned that an effective means of identification is only as good as the practitioners and the methodology associated with that form of identification.

Early Nonsystematic Methods of Identification

Criminal identification is an age-old problem. That is, how might one individual be identified sufficiently to separate that individual from others? Early mankind had no way to use a systematic method to identify an individual. What was utilized? Simple recognition was the method. This was a crude form of *classification: Starting with the largest unit* (the group) *and separating point by point* (recognition) *until the desired subject is remaining* (the individual). As time progressed and mankind became a bit more learned, better methods were chosen to distinguish one person from another. But the central question remained: How does one describe another so others will recognize the individual being described? *The ideal identification system enables the orator or operator to say with a high degree of certainty that the subject is the desired person.*

From the perspective of tribal man, the manner in which individuals were identified was simple association and recognition. These were non-mobile societies, so most individuals knew one another. Those individuals traveled in the same groups for gathering, hunting, socialization, and protection. Obviously, it was much easier to recognize members of the group than it was to distinguish individual outsiders.

As time evolved, and for specificity, the tribes or groups began to consciously alter their appearance to set them apart from others. This was accomplished through intentional or unintentional infliction of specific markings on the individuals such as scars or disfigurement. As the tribe or family wanted to set itself apart from others, it became commonplace for that family to mark itself with the likes of caste marks, tattoos, or even simple tribal dress. For those who offended the group, intentional mutilation was chosen for wrongdoing to mark those persons who were outcasts. Mutilation was carried out in the form of altering offending limbs, changing facial features, or in some instances, amputation. Other methods of distinguishing an individual were to brand the individual with a specific mark, possibly denoting a specific offense. Some emerging countries throughout the world still use this manner of individualization as a form of punishment today. As the sophistication of tribes grew and they developed into communities and societies, the need for identification became more pronounced as the issue of mobility came to the forefront. Forced transportation from one country to another became another issue to distinguish individuals. Many of the methods of identification in the New World or new colonies were borrowed from the already entrenched societies. Newer, more humane methods to mark or identify individuals were seen in the form of mechanical devices such as stocks and boots, or public humiliation in the form of sitting or being placed in a basket or swinging in the public square. All of these methods served a purpose when taken in context of the times. One other distinguishing attribute that we often do not think about is that of language. The language spoken, the type of dialect, and any specific nuances that may be used in speaking are powerful forms of identification. How often has it been said that two people are speaking the same language but cannot understand each other? Again, this example is a method of distinguishing one individual from another due to a specific trait.

Today we know that a mistake-proof method of identification is required. Due to the mobility of our societies, a method of identification that can provide an absolute identification within minutes is required. The anonymity of society today necessitates a reliable method of identifying someone. Simply put, how many of you really know your neighbors?

Anonymity has become commonplace in many societies worldwide. We can see that today, more so than any other time in history, the necessity of identifying and apprehending a wrongdoer swiftly and accurately is paramount and a necessary part of our criminal justice system. No longer can we afford to be complacent as the potential damage to the greater society can be enormous. For example, with the availability of modern modes of transportation, an individual who commits a crime, if not apprehended in short order, may be in another jurisdiction, state, or country within a matter of minutes or hours.

Never in the history of mankind has the ability to identify and individualize a person been greater than it is today. The amount of

The History of Fingerprints

destruction and carnage that can be inflicted by one individual necessitates an excellent, systematic method of identification. We, as a worldwide criminal identification community, are required by the times to do all in our power to identify criminal perpetrators and victims of crime, as well as to possess the ability to assist in civil disasters. The task of the criminal identification specialist or practitioner is an ongoing process that remains, at times, overwhelming. We must strive to persevere.

> Without studying the basics, one cannot comprehend the complex.
> —Author unknown

Chapter 1 Study Questions

1. What evidence exists that fingerprints were understood to be unique to the individual in ancient times?
2. What do we mean when we say that identification is based on classification?
3. What are the Galton details?
4. What contribution did each of the following individuals make to the science of fingerprints?
    a. Nehemiah Grew
    b. J.C.A. Mayer
    c. Johannes Purkinje
    d. Sir William Herschel
    e. Dr. Henry Faulds
    f. Juan Vucetich
    g. Sir Francis Galton
    h. Sir Edward Henry
    i. Sgt. John Ferrier
    j. Mary E. Holland
5. What was the recommendation of the Belper Commission?
6. Explain why there was a reluctance to accept fingerprints as an absolute method of identification in the early years.
7. An ideal identification system serves to do what?
8. Who is credited with the first criminal identification through the use of fingerprints?
9. Name the various methods of identification prior to Bertillon.
10. The study of fingerprints is similar to any other science. What does that statement mean?

Systematic Methods of Identification

2

The first real method of identification was the artist's rendering. Drawing a picture of what was seen by another individual is not an easy task. The challenge has always been to relay the information in such a way that it is understandable to the person who is doing the sketch. There have always been those individuals who have used their creativity to generate a likeness of an individual. As standardized terminology and descriptors were developed, the quality of the sketch was remarkably improved. Today, we commonly refer to this method as a police artist sketch. The problem that has always existed with an artist's rendering is the ability of the artist to put onto paper what one individual has put into words to describe another individual. *An artist's rendering is never going to produce or replicate an exact likeness of an individual.* That is why, even today, the police sketch is, at best, a very close likeness of an individual. Coming in a close second, due to the lateness of its development, is the photograph. A photograph, as we know, will produce an exact likeness of an individual. The first such device for photography was the *Daguerreotype* that was first used in Brussels around 1843. A photograph was developed on a light-sensitive silver-coated metallic plate. Later, a glass plate was used. This method, to say the least, was extremely cumbersome as the photographs that were taken were not extremely high quality, and the equipment associated with the task made it difficult at best to take photographs in a less than controlled environment. As time has evolved, these techniques or processes were replaced with cellulose acetate, commonly referred to as camera film. As with all inventions or technology, photographic technology has become very sophisticated, easy to use, and for the most part, inexpensive. That is why the portable camera has made the job of photographic documentation so much easier and desirable. However, with film, there was still one major drawback: one could not instantly see the photograph one was trying to capture. Newer technology, such as Polaroid instant cameras, soon filled the void of immediacy. However, with immediacy of the photograph, certain sacrifices had to be made such as quality and longevity. The photos taken with the Polaroid-type cameras could not capture quality depth of field and the photos were not long-lasting. As the technology evolved, so too have the types of cameras, to the point that today we have good-quality digital cameras that allow us to immediately view that we have just photographed. If the photograph does not capture sufficient information, another photograph can be immediately taken. The quality and affordability of the digital camera are attainable by most law enforcement and governmental agencies today. It is also said that film, as we know it today, will be replaced with digital photography due to cost, dependability, usability, and storage. However, cameras are not always present during the commission of crimes, although that is changing with the advent of the mini-cam or the video/digital recorder, as well as the ubiquitous digital phone. An ideal systematic method of identification combines the features of a sketch, a photograph, and other methodology to document the specificity of an individual, a location, or an event.

The first such documented system, which combined the photograph and physical description, was a system developed by Alphonse Bertillon, circa 1883 (Figure 2.1). This system became known as Bertillonage or anthropometry. The system consisted of four parts: anthropometry (body measurements), *portrait parlé* (spoken picture or verbal description), photographs, and fingerprints.

Bertillonage

Anthropometry consisted of taking specific body measurements metrically and classifying those measurements into small, medium, and large. That information was then recorded and placed on index cards and filed. The body measurements consisted of the length of arms, sitting height, caliper measurements of the head, right arm, left foot, left middle finger, left forearm, and right ear. While measuring women, measurements of the head, left foot, and elbow were excluded. For boys and young men, classification was according to the color of eyes and details of ears.

Bertillon set down the principles of anthropometry. The principles stated:

1. The human skeleton is unchangeable after the 20th year. (Thigh bones grow but the spine curves to compensate.)
2. It is impossible to find two human bones exactly alike.
3. Necessary measurements could easily be taken with the aid of simple instruments (calipers; Figure 2.2)

Figure 2.1 Alphonse Bertillon.

The other part of Bertillonage was known as *portrait parlé*, which literally means "spoken picture" or physical description. This part of the system consisted of four parts:

1. *Determination of color* of the left eye, hair, beard, and skin.
2. *Morphological determinators* such as shape, direction, and size of every part of the head.
3. *General determinators* such as grade of stoutness, carriage, voice, language, dress, social standing, height, and weight.
4. *Description of indelible marks* such as birthmarks, scars, and tattoos.

Bertillon also required the use of a full face and profile photo that were affixed to the cards. Finally, Bertillon affixed fingerprints to the rear of the index cards; however, Bertillon always championed his anthropometry as a means of identification. Oddly enough, it was fingerprints, which Bertillon recorded, that were responsible for the ultimate demise of the anthropometrical system.

Shortcomings of the Bertillon system of identification were the cause of the demise of the system in its totality. Examination of the Bertillon system reveals the following shortcomings:

1. The system was *limited to adults*, as the theory espoused by Bertillon said the skeleton remained unchanged after the 20th year. What

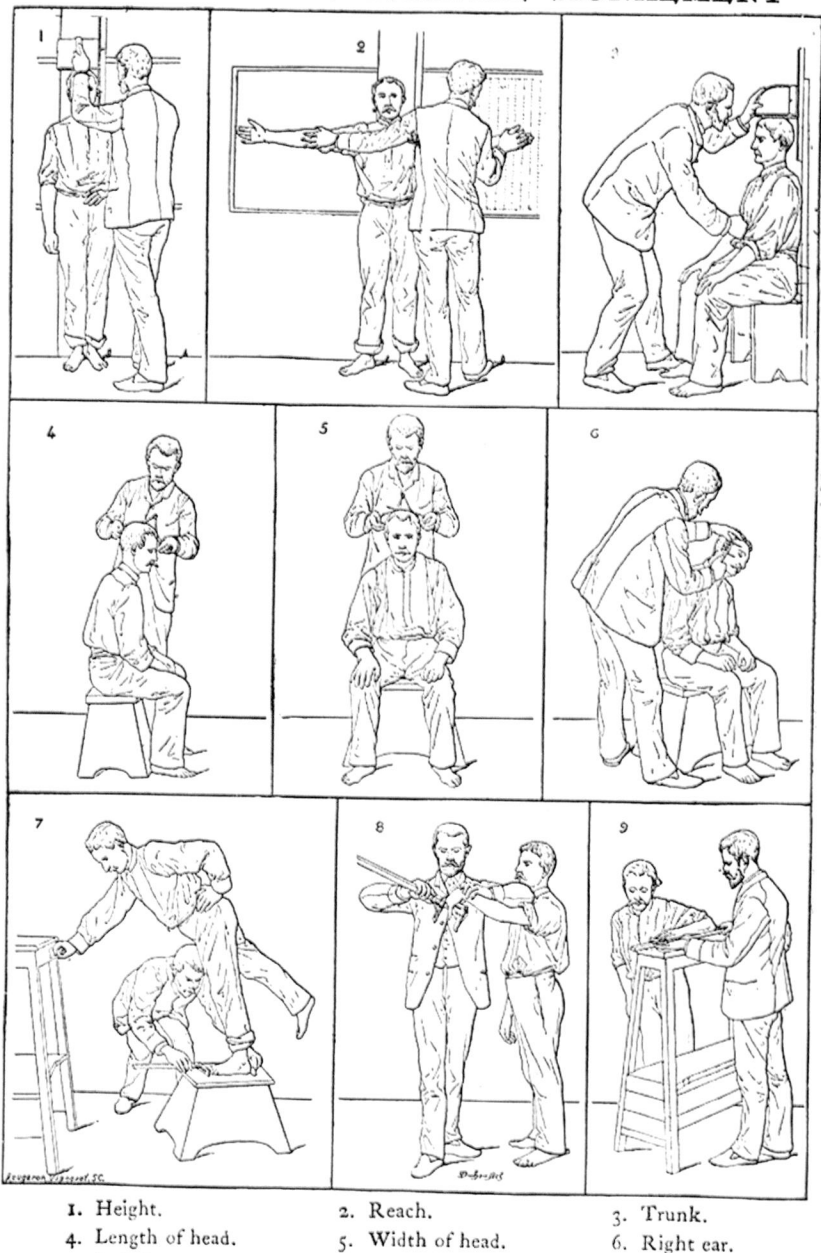

Figure 2.2 Body measurements for the Bertillon method.

Systematic Methods of Identification

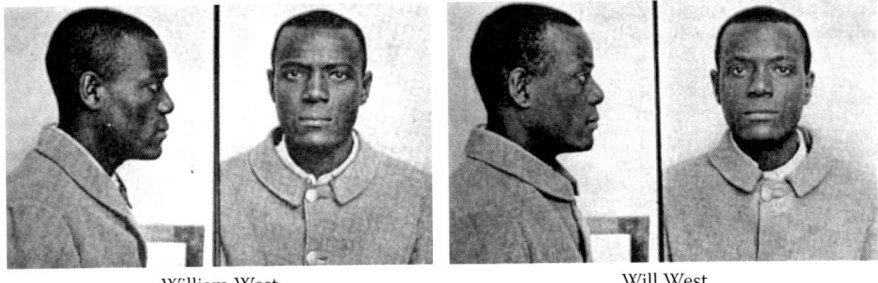

William West   Will West

Figure 2.3 The West case: William West and Will West.

about those persons under the age of twenty? Although provisions were made for children, the provisions proved insignificant.
2. The system was often marked by *significant differences in measurements* of the same criminal by different examiners. As with any repetitious task, often the practitioner became complacent and was not as vigilant as one would desire.
3. Soft property of the ears resulted in that portion of anthropometry being dropped.
4. The system was *extremely slow* (measuring devices consisted of calipers and similar measuring devices, which in and of themselves were laborious to use).
5. The *West Case* of Ft. Leavenworth, Kansas, 1903. Will West was sentenced to prison, and when being processed was accused of being William West on the basis of his physical appearance and anthropometrical measurements. William West was called from the prison population where he was serving a life sentence for murder. The appearance of the two men was striking and their physical attributes were identical (Figure 2.3). Fingerprints were then taken in an attempt to determine identity. When compared, the prints did not match. Were they two twins who had never met? The two Wests were African Americans and it has been speculated that they may have been the offspring of slaves, separated at birth, and had never met until this fateful day.

Although there were shortcomings to the Bertillon system, there were values established that are still in use today. The values established by Bertillonage were:

1. Establishment of a full face/profile fixed-scale photograph. (Today the addition of numbers on the photographs serve as an additional identification marker.)

2. Establishment of the use of a detailed description (*portrait parlé*/ physical description). (General descriptors such as height, weight, race, age, and specific descriptors such as scars, marks, and tattoos are used.)
3. Establishment of the concept of repeated subdivision of data for ease of filing and searching (gathering information and categorizing it in a systematic form).
4. Demonstration that fingerprints could be used to individualize identity.

Although Bertillon promoted the idea of a systematic method of identification, the shortcomings of his system gave rise to what would become the most widely used method of identification and individualization worldwide for the next eighty years: fingerprints. Technology did not come to the forefront for purposes of individualization through bodily fluids until the 1980s with the advent of the use of *deoxyribonucleic acid* (DNA).

Fingerprints

The use of fingerprints began in earnest as a method of identification in the late 1800s and early 1900s with the establishment of fingerprint classification systems. To thoroughly understand fingerprint identification and the methodology associated with the process, it is necessary to understand the terminology associated with fingerprints that has been established. Let us begin by setting forth definitions associated with fingerprints.

Definitions Associated with Fingerprints

Historical terms associated with fingerprints come from various parts of the world.

> *Dactylography*, a Greek term that translates as "finger writing."
> *Dactyloscopy*, a Greek term that translates as "to view the fingers."
> *Dermatoglyphics*, a Latin term that translates as "skin carving."

How, one might ask, do these terms apply to fingerprints? The terms are all associated with the fingers in one way or another and demonstrate that the pursuit of knowledge of fingerprints has been around for centuries. The modern day equivalent or usage of these terms can be converted into *the scientific study of fingerprints for the purpose of identification.*

How is a fingerprint defined? The following definitions will assist in understanding what we call a fingerprint, palm print, or footprint.

Systematic Methods of Identification

Fingerprint—The impression or reproduction left on any material by the friction skin of the fingers. Most often we see the impression left by the fingertips or the bulb of the fingers. But the friction skin covers the entire area of the inner hand (the palm) and fingers.

Palm print—The impression or reproduction left on any material by the friction skin of the palms.

Footprint/toe print—The impression or reproduction left on any material by the friction skin of the foot (feet) or toe(s).

It should be noted that friction skin is found on the hands and the feet of individuals. The *friction skin* is the outer layer of skin that contains many of the elements and characteristics we use to identify and individualize a print.

Friction skin—The skin on the inner hands and fingers, and on the bottom of the feet and toes, which is characterized by alternating strips of raised ridges and furrows arranged in a variety of patterns. The friction skin is found on both humans and anthropoids. In lower mammals, friction ridge patterns are sometimes similar to ours. Friction surfaces are sometimes padded in apes. The purpose of the friction skin, as the name implies, is to provide resistance so that those surfaces containing friction skin will be able to grasp objects. The friction skin forms during the third or fourth month of fetal growth (approximately 120 days). The process by which friction skin develops is through the formation of small islands surrounding pores, which then develop to form ridges.

Friction ridge—The raised portion of the skin that leaves the impression or reproduction.

Furrow—The portion of the skin lower and between the ridges.

A cross-section of friction skin (Figure 2.4) illustrates various parts and layers of the skin.

1. Epidermal layer: Outer layer
    a. Stratum corneum: Surface skin
        i. Friction ridges, furrows, and pores
        ii. 1- to 2-mm thick
    b. Stratum mucosum (Malpighi—inner skin)
        i. Programs/forms outer skin

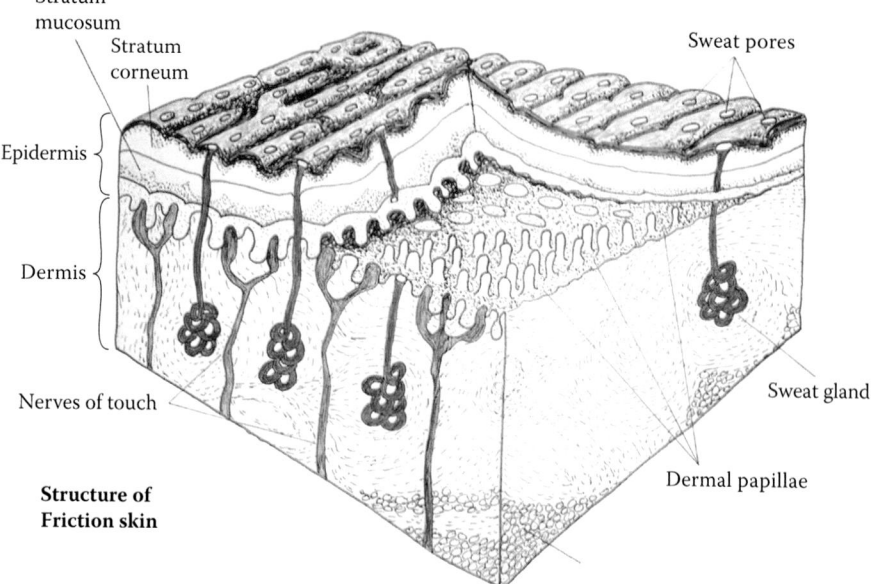

Figure 2.4 Cross-section of the structure of friction skin.

   2. Dermal layer: (inner layer/second layer)
      a. Dermal papillae
         i. Determines ridge structure
      b. Sweat glands and ducts
      c. Nerves of touch (sensors)
      d. Fat

The *constancy (persistence)* and *uniqueness of friction ridges* are:

Friction skin is persistent. That is, the skin does not change under normal conditions from the time of formation until decomposition after death. The exception is that, like other parts of the anatomy, the fingerprints or friction skin will get larger as the body grows. However, the specific characteristics will remain the same. Friction skin will deteriorate with age as well as all skin, but classification and identification normally will not be affected. There is an adage that is often used to describe the persistence: *under normal wear and tear, friction skin will remain unchanged throughout one's life.*

Friction skin destruction (temporary or persistent) encompasses: An injury penetrating into the dermal layer (second layer of skin), through the dermal papillae, will result in the ridges not being regenerated. Scar tissue will form to the extent that the damage occurred, and only those ridges in the path of the injury should be permanently affected.

Injuries to the epidermal layer (first or outer layer) will repair themselves as they were prior to the injury, for example, paper cuts.

There are many instances in legend where allegedly people have sanded, burned, or surgically altered their fingerprints with persistent results. Research has demonstrated what effect different techniques have on the appearance of fingerprints.

Self-induced injuries cannot remove all ridges or the hands would be too severely injured to be used. What one must understand is that friction ridges cover the entire surface of the inner hands and bottom of the feet.

If the pattern area alone were disfigured, classification might be affected, but identification or individualization would not. In all likelihood, the pattern would be made more unique, which would make identification and individualization that much easier.

Other alterations to the friction skin whether it be surgical, occupational, or medical can have an impact on the appearance. Examples are as follows:

Skin grafts would result in either the old pattern being regenerated as the graft skin wore away or the graft area remaining smooth. A new pattern would not occur.

Occupational wear might wear down the ridges, but the cessation of the work will result in the ridges becoming distinct again.

Disease can have an effect on fingerprints as well; such as in the latter stages of leprosy, the skin may flake off and the pattern may be lost. Allergic reactions may have an effect on the ridges in that a temporary change may occur but when the reaction disappears, ridges should return to their configuration. Other conditions such as warts, creases, or calluses may be present but seldom affect classification and rarely, if ever, affect identification.

Based on the foundation and fundamentals of the aforementioned information, a *basis of the science of fingerprints* was established:

1. Every finger contains ridge detail that is unique to that finger and no other.
2. Unique ridge details do not change (except in size) from approximately one hundred twenty days after conception until decomposition after death.

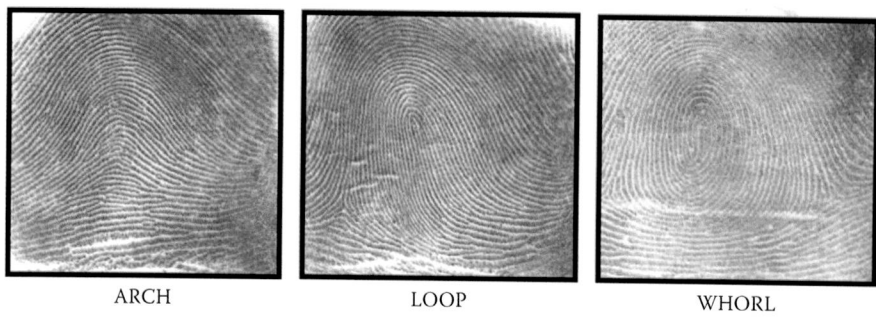

Figure 2.5 Fingerprint patterns (Source: NIST).

3. A set of fingerprints lends itself to classification and therefore can be filed and searched. Whether the system be manual or automated does not matter.

   Fingerprint classification—The process of assigning a formula, consisting of numbers and letters, to a set of fingerprints determined by the pattern interpretation and ridge detail of the fingerprints themselves.

   Fingerprint identification (individualization)—The process of determining that the same finger made two or more impressions based on the friction ridge details of both impressions (to the exclusion of all others).

Fingerprint Patterns and Ridge Characteristics

There are three main types of fingerprint patterns with several subgroups of patterns:

1. Arch patterns account for approximately 5–15 percent of fingerprint patterns. Arch patterns can be further categorized into two subgroups:
   a. Plain arches
   b. Tented arches

2. Loop patterns account for 60–65 percent of fingerprint patterns. The loop pattern is the most common. There are two subgroups (automated systems simply use the terms right slant or left slant):
   a. Ulnar (ridges flow toward the little finger)
   b. Radial (ridges flow toward the thumb)

Systematic Methods of Identification

3. Whorl patterns account for 30–35 percent of fingerprint patterns. Whorls can further be categorized into four subgroups:
    a. Plain
    b. Double loop—sometimes called lateral loops
    c. Central pocket loop
    d. Accidental

Ridge characteristics or Galton details may take the following forms:

1. Staple or recurve
2. Convergence
3. Appendage
4. Bifurcation
5. Divergence
6. Rod enclosed in recurving
7. Enclosure or island
8. Dot
9. Short ridge
10. Long ridge
11. Incipient ridges
12. Ending ridge

More Fingerprint Definitions

Pattern area—That part of a loop or whorl pattern in which appear the cores, deltas, and ridges, which we are concerned with in classifying. (The pattern areas of loops and whorls are enclosed by type lines—a plain arch pattern is often referred to as an *absence of pattern* due to the lack of deltas, type lines, or a defined core.)

Type lines—The two innermost ridges that start parallel, diverge, and surround or tend to surround the pattern area (Figure 2.6).

Core—The approximate center of the fingerprint pattern. (A loop pattern has specific rules governing choices between cores.)

The delta—The delta is that point on a ridge at or in front of and nearest the center of the divergence of the type lines (Figure 2.6).

What is the importance of fingerprints or how can fingerprints be used? Fingerprints can be used for both criminal and noncriminal purposes. In criminal matters, the obvious uses are to place a suspect at a scene of a crime, or to place or associate possession of a particular item with a suspect. This assists in the investigation by proving or disproving a set of facts or

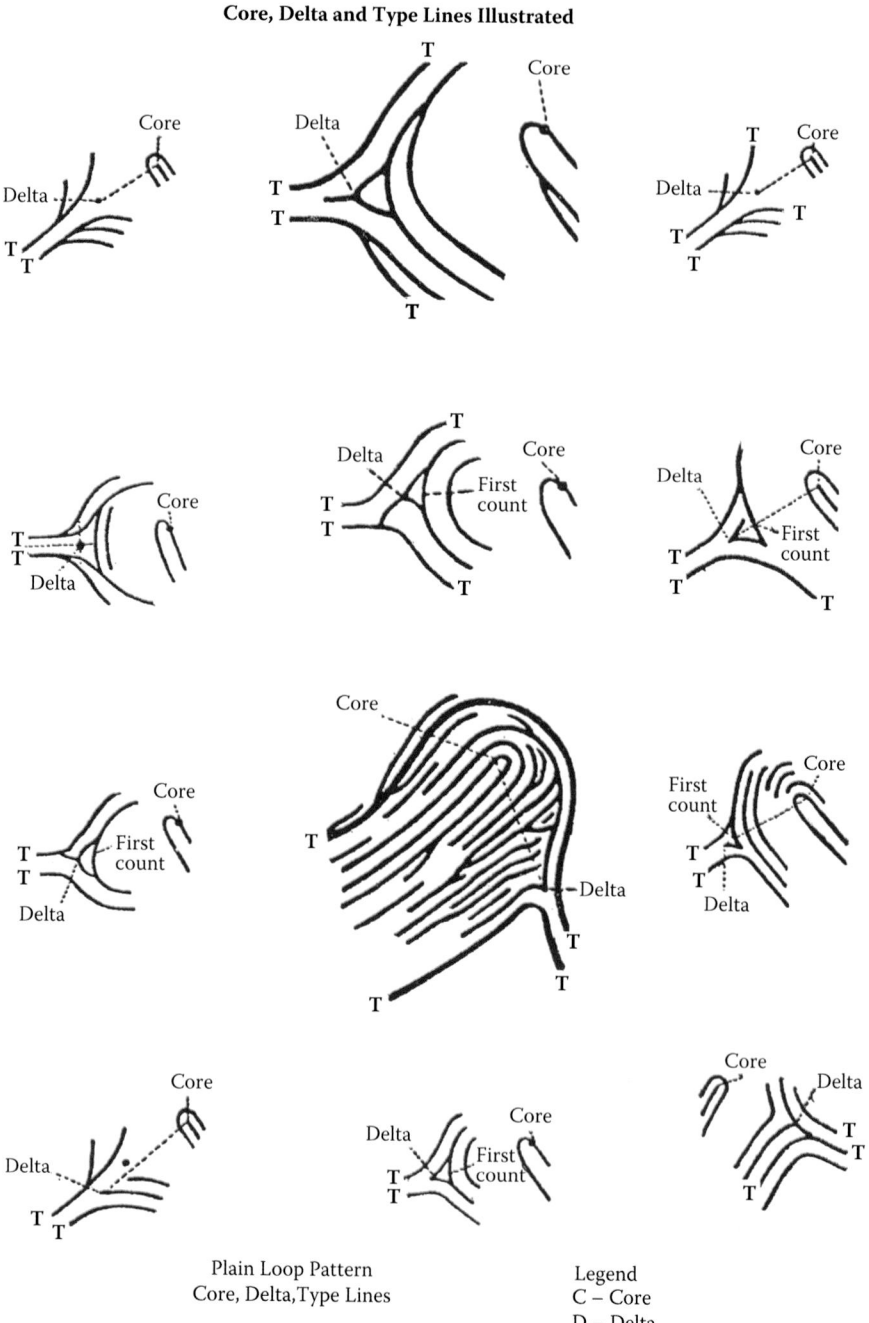

Figure 2.6 Plain loop pattern; core, delta, and type lines illustrated: C, core; D, delta; T, type lines.

circumstances. Fingerprint evidence can also serve to corroborate information or statements. In noncriminal matters, commonly referred as civil matters, fingerprints are of use for identification purposes in disasters. Unfortunately, fingerprints cannot be used in all instances. Forensic odontology or DNA profiling may be utilized in those instances where fingerprints cannot be used. However, because of the ease of use and understanding, as well as the speed with which fingerprints can be used, fingerprints are the first choice of many experts.

Other issues that are important to include in fingerprint discussion:

There is strong evidence that fingerprint patterns tend to run in families.

A *bifurcation* is the forking or the dividing of one ridge into two or more ridges (Figure 2.6).

A *divergence* is the spreading apart of two ridges that have been running parallel or nearly parallel (Figure 2.6).

Finally, angles are never formed by a single ridge but by the abutting of one ridge against another (two ridges involved). Therefore, an angular formation can never be used as a type line. *Focal points* or *target areas* are those areas within the pattern that contain ridge characteristics (Galton details) which are used for comparison and classification. (Galton details or ridge characteristics are contained in the second level of the comparison process. This level is discussed in the material on conducting fingerprint comparisons.)

Chapter 2 Study Questions

1. What is anthropometry?
2. What are the principles on which anthropometry is based?
3. What are the components of the Bertillon system?
4. What are the components of *portrait parlé* as devised by Bertillon?
5. What are the values of the Bertillon system?
6. What are the shortcomings of the Bertillon system?
7. What was the West case, and what impact or effect did it have on criminal identification?
8. What is meant by the term *portrait parlé*?
9. Has the use of fingerprinting made *portrait parlé* obsolete?
10. What do the terms dactylography, dermatoglyphics, and dactyloscopy mean?
11. What is a fingerprint?

12. What is the friction skin?
13. When is the friction skin formed?
14. What is a friction ridge? A furrow?
15. What is the basis for the science of fingerprints?
16. Define fingerprint identification.
17. Define the pattern area.
18. Identify the various ridge characteristics.
19. What are the types of fingerprint patterns (the main types and subtypes)?
20. Define fingerprint classification.

Fingerprint Pattern Types and Associated Terminology

3

Loop Pattern

Definition: A loop is that type of fingerprint pattern in which one or more of the ridges enter on either side of the impression; recurve, touch, or pass an imaginary line drawn from the delta to the core; and terminate or tend to terminate on or toward the same side of the impression from which such ridge or ridges entered (Figures 3.1 through 3.18).

Requirements of a loop: A loop pattern must possess the following essentials:

- A delta
- A sufficient recurve
- One or more ridge count across a looping ridge

A *sufficient recurve* can be defined as that part of a recurving ridge between the shoulders of a loop that is free of any appendages abutting upon the outside of the recurve at right angles.

The delta:

- A delta may be:
  - Bifurcation—To be chosen, the bifurcation must open toward the core
  - An abrupt ending ridge
  - A dot
  - A short ridge

- A meeting of two ridges
- A point on the first recurving ridge located nearest to the center and in front of the divergence of the type lines.

- Rules governing the choice between two deltas:
  - When there is a choice between a bifurcation and another type of delta, the bifurcation is selected.
  - When there are two or more possible deltas that conform to the definition, the one nearest to the core is chosen.
  - The delta may not be located in the middle of a ridge running between the type lines toward the core, but at the nearer end only.
  - If the ridge is entirely in the pattern area, the delta is placed on the end nearer to the divergence.
  - If the ridge enters the pattern area from a point below the divergence, the delta is located at the end nearest to the core.

The core:

- Rules governing selection
  - The core is placed on or within the innermost sufficient recurve.
  - The shoulders of a loop are the points at which the recurving ridge definitely turns inward or recurves. The core is placed inside the shoulders (Figure 3.19).
  - When the innermost sufficient recurve contains no ending ridge or rod rising as high as the shoulders of the loop, the core is placed on the shoulder of the loop farther from the delta (Figure 3.20).
  - If both shoulders are equidistant to the delta, the core is then located on the center of the sufficient recurve (Figure 3.21).
  - When the innermost sufficient recurve contains an uneven number of rods rising as high as the shoulders, the core is placed on the end of the center rod whether it touches the looping ridge or not (Figure 3.22).
  - When the innermost sufficient recurve contains an even number of rods rising as high as the shoulders, the core is placed on the end of the farther of the two center rods (farther from the delta). The two center rods are treated as though they were connected by a recurving ridge (Figure 3.23).

Fingerprint Pattern Types and Terminology

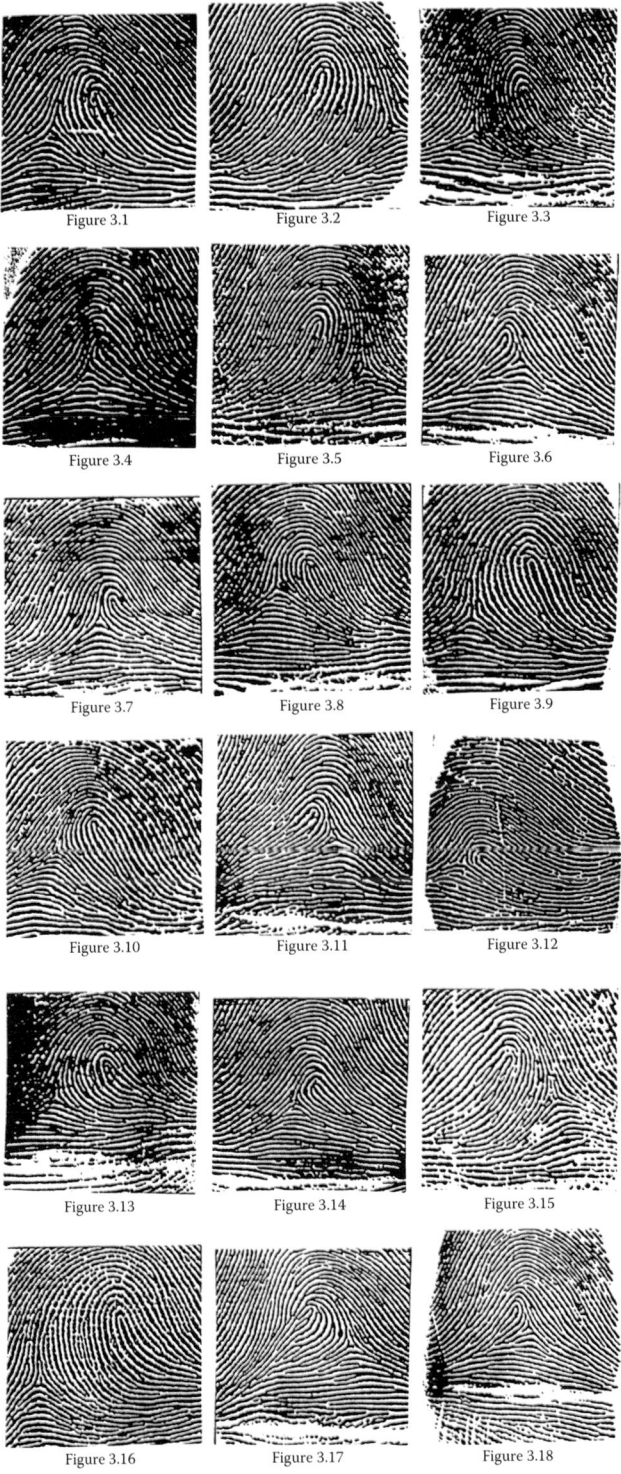

Figure 3.1
Figure 3.2
Figure 3.3
Figure 3.4
Figure 3.5
Figure 3.6
Figure 3.7
Figure 3.8
Figure 3.9
Figure 3.10
Figure 3.11
Figure 3.12
Figure 3.13
Figure 3.14
Figure 3.15
Figure 3.16
Figure 3.17
Figure 3.18

Figure 3.1–3.18

Figure 3.19

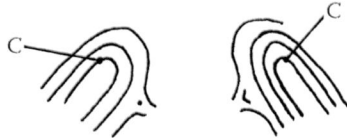

Figure 3.20

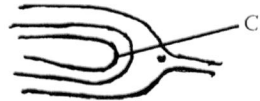

Figure 3.21

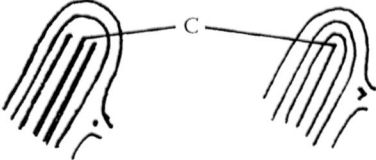

Figure 3.22

- The recurve must have no appendages abutting upon it at right angles between the shoulders and on the outside. If such appendage is present, the loop is considered spoiled and the next loop outside will be considered to locate the core (Figure 3.24).

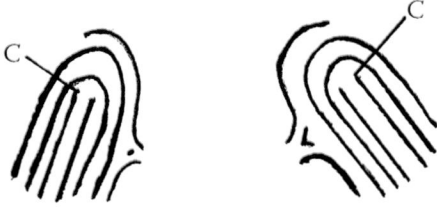

Figure 3.23

Fingerprint Pattern Types and Terminology

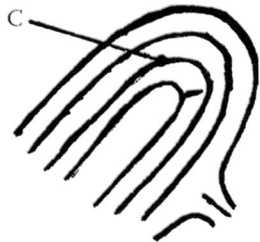

Figure 3.24

- Loops at the center of the pattern
    - Interlocking loops (Figure 3.25)
    - Two loops (Figure 3.26)
- Examples of incomplete loops where an essential element is missing
    - Recurve missing (Figure 3.27)
    - Delta missing (Figure 3.28)
    - Ridge count missing (Figure 3.29)
- Where an essential element of a loop is missing, the pattern will be classified as a tented arch.

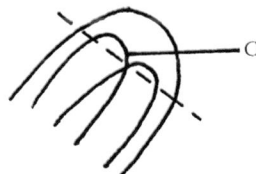

Figure 3.25

Figure 3.26

Figure 3.27

Loop Ridge Counting

Ridge counting defined: The number of ridges intervening between the delta and the core (Figure 3.19).

Procedure for ridge counting: An imaginary line is placed between the core and the delta. Each ridge that crosses or touches the line is counted.

1. The delta and core are not counted.
2. Where the line touches a ridge at the point of bifurcation, two ridges are counted.
3. Where the line crosses an island, both sides are counted.
4. Fragments and dots are counted only if they appear to be as thick and heavy as other ridges in the pattern (Figure 3.30).
5. A white space *must* intervene between the delta and the first ridge count, or the first ridge must be disregarded.
6. When the core is located on a spike that touches the inside of the innermost recurving ridge, the recurve is included in the ridge count only when the delta is located below a line drawn at right angles.

Figure 3.28

Fingerprint Pattern Types and Terminology

Figure 3.29

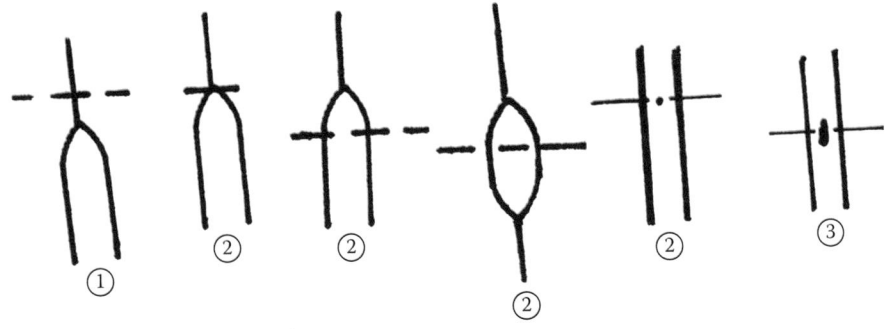

Figure 3.30

    a. Counted (Figure 3.31)
    b. Not counted (Figure 3.32)

Radial and Ulnar Loops

1. The terms have been derived from the radial and ulnar bones of the forearm.

Figure 3.31

Figure 3.32

    a. Loops flowing in the direction of the little finger are ulnar loops.
    b. Loops flowing in the direction of the thumb are radial loops.
        i. Fingerprint cards: (manual/live scan)
        ii. Right hand: Position as on the hand
        iii. Left hand: The reverse
    c. For purposes of automated use, loops are termed either *right slanted* (those patterns where ridges flow to the right) or *left slanted* (those patterns where ridges flow to the left).
2. Determining the direction of flow:
    a. Begin at the core and follow or trace the ridges away from the delta.
    b. From the recurve to the open end of loop.

Other Issues Pertaining to Loops

1. ***Sufficient recurve:*** The part of a recurving ridge between the shoulders of a loop. It must be free of any appendage abutting upon the outside of the recurve at right angles.
2. If a ridge enters on one side of the impression, recurves, and passes an imaginary line drawn between the delta and core but does not terminate on the side from which it entered, *but has a tendency to do so*, the pattern is a loop (Figure 3.34).
3. The recurve may take unusual forms (Figure 3.35).
4. The recurving ridge does not begin at the edge of the print, but possesses all the requirements of the loop (Figure 3.36).
5. The recurving ridge enters from one side, recurves, and turns back on itself. This is a loop pattern (Figure 3.37).

Fingerprint Pattern Types and Terminology 37

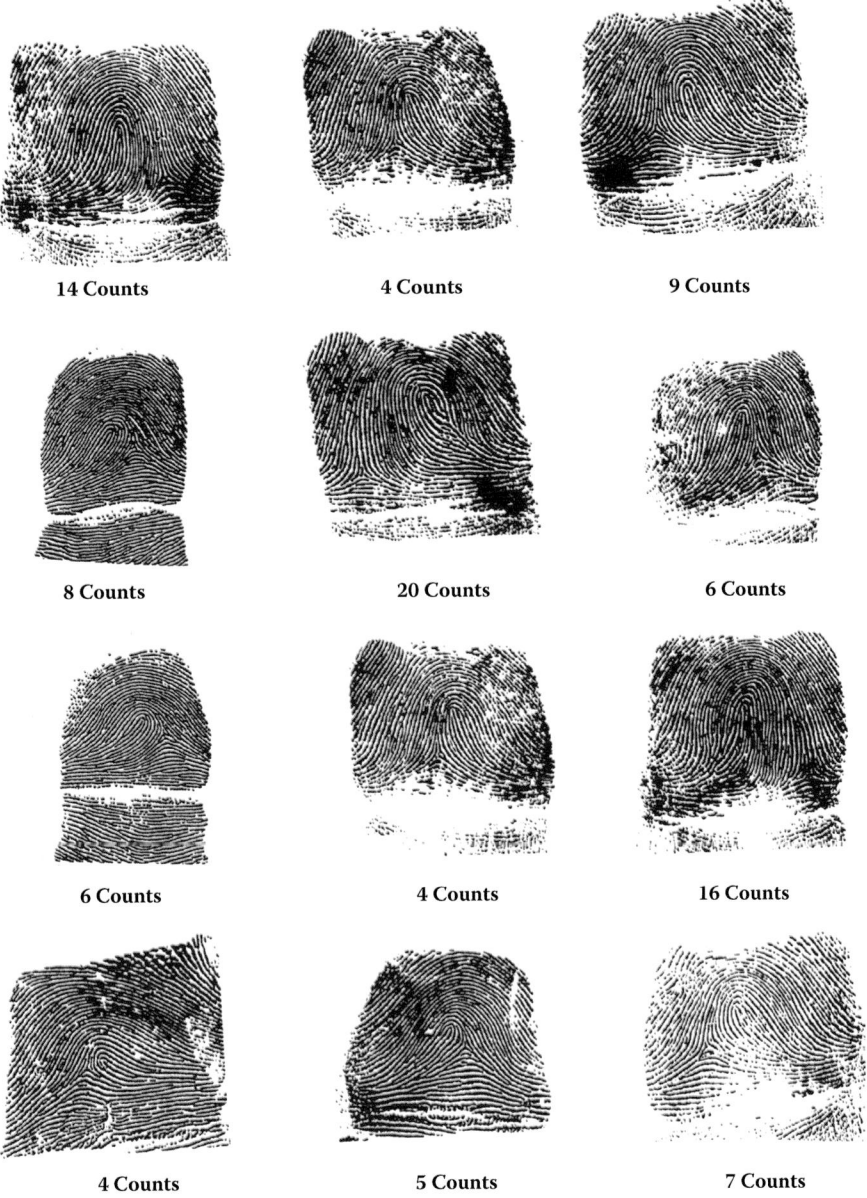

Figure 3.33 Loop ridge counts.

Figure 3.34

Figure 3.35

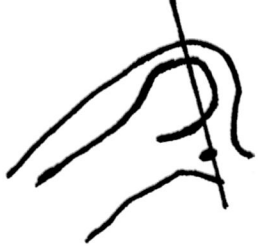

Figure 3.36

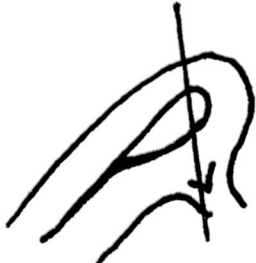

Figure 3.37

Fingerprint Pattern Types and Terminology

Plain Arch and Tented Arch Patterns

The Plain Arch

Definition: The ridges enter on one side of the impression and flow or tend to flow out the other with a rise or wave in the center. There may be various ridge formations such as ending ridges, bifurcations, dots, and so forth, but they all tend to follow the general ridge contour. The *"crest"* of an arch is the highest point reached by the rising friction ridge. Most often that will be in the middle of the friction ridge. The plain arch is also known as an absence of pattern (the plain arch has no delta, no real core as in a loop, nor can a ridge tracing be conducted as in a whorl pattern) (Figures 3.38 through 3.46).

The Tented Arch

Definition: Most of the ridges enter on one side of the impression and flow or tend to flow out on the other side, as in the plain arch; however, the ridge or ridges at the center do not (Figures 3.47 through 3.55).

1. There are three types of tented arches.
   a. The type in which ridges at the center form a definite angle of 90 degrees or less (Figure 3.74).
   b. The type in which one or more ridges at the center form an upthrust. An upthrust is an ending ridge of any length rising at a sufficient degree from the horizontal plane, that is, 45 degrees or more (Figure 3.75).
   c. The type approaching the loop, possessing two of the three basic essential characteristics, but lacking the third.
      i. The mere converging of two ridges does not form a recurve, without which there can be no loop.
      ii. The presence of the slightest upthrust at the center of the impression is sufficient to make the pattern a tented arch.
      iii. The upthrust must be an ending ridge. It cannot be a continuation of a curving ridge. Test for upthrust: If the ridges on both sides of the ending ridge follow direction or flow trend of the upthrust, the print may be classed as a P/A. If, however, the ridges on only one side follow its direction, it is a T/A.
      iv. An appendage or spike abutting upon a recurve at right angles in the space between the shoulders of a loop on the outside is considered to spoil the recurve.

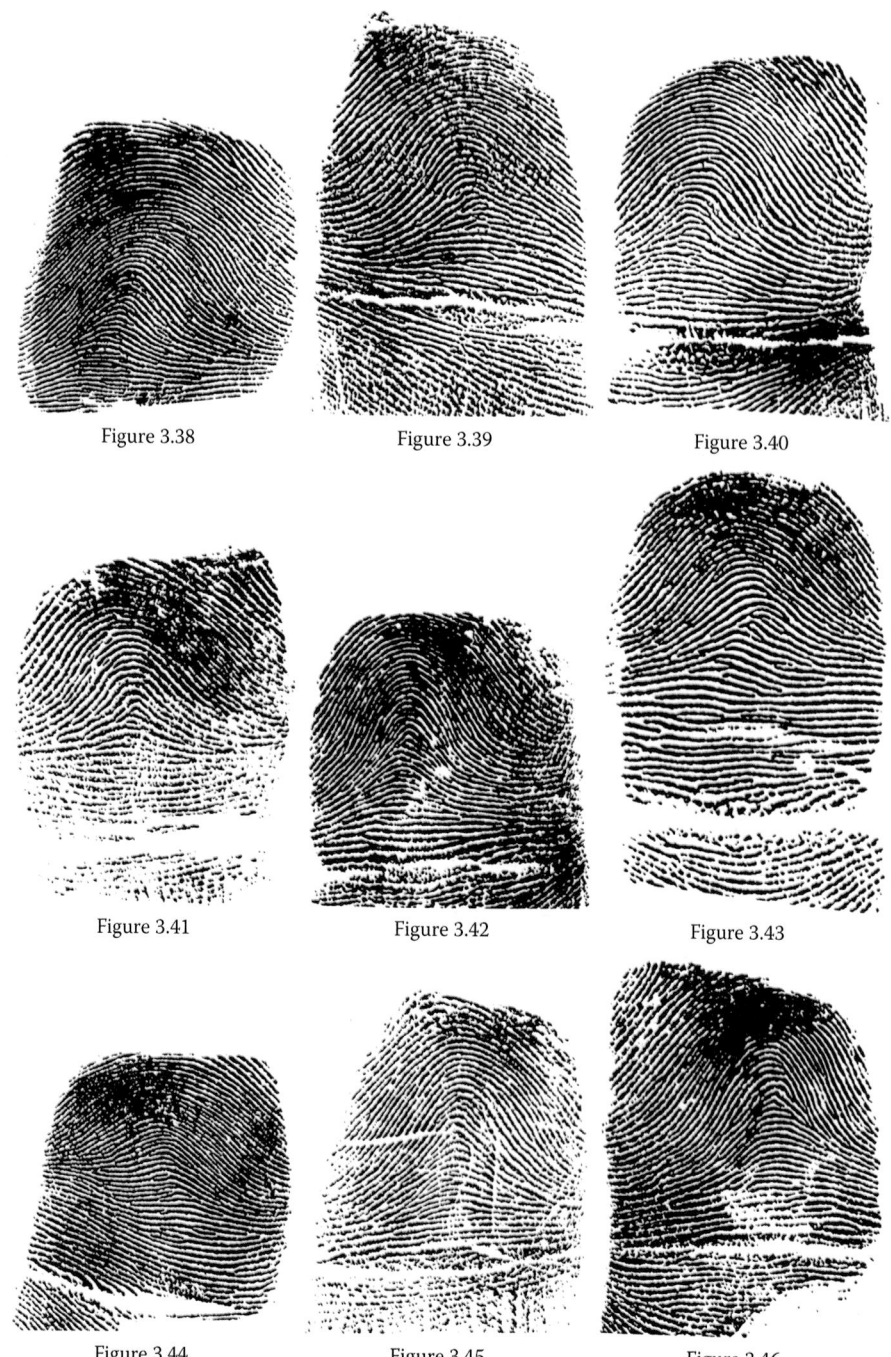

Figure 3.38

Figure 3.39

Figure 3.40

Figure 3.41

Figure 3.42

Figure 3.43

Figure 3.44

Figure 3.45

Figure 3.46

Figure 3.38–3.46 Plain arch patterns.

Fingerprint Pattern Types and Terminology

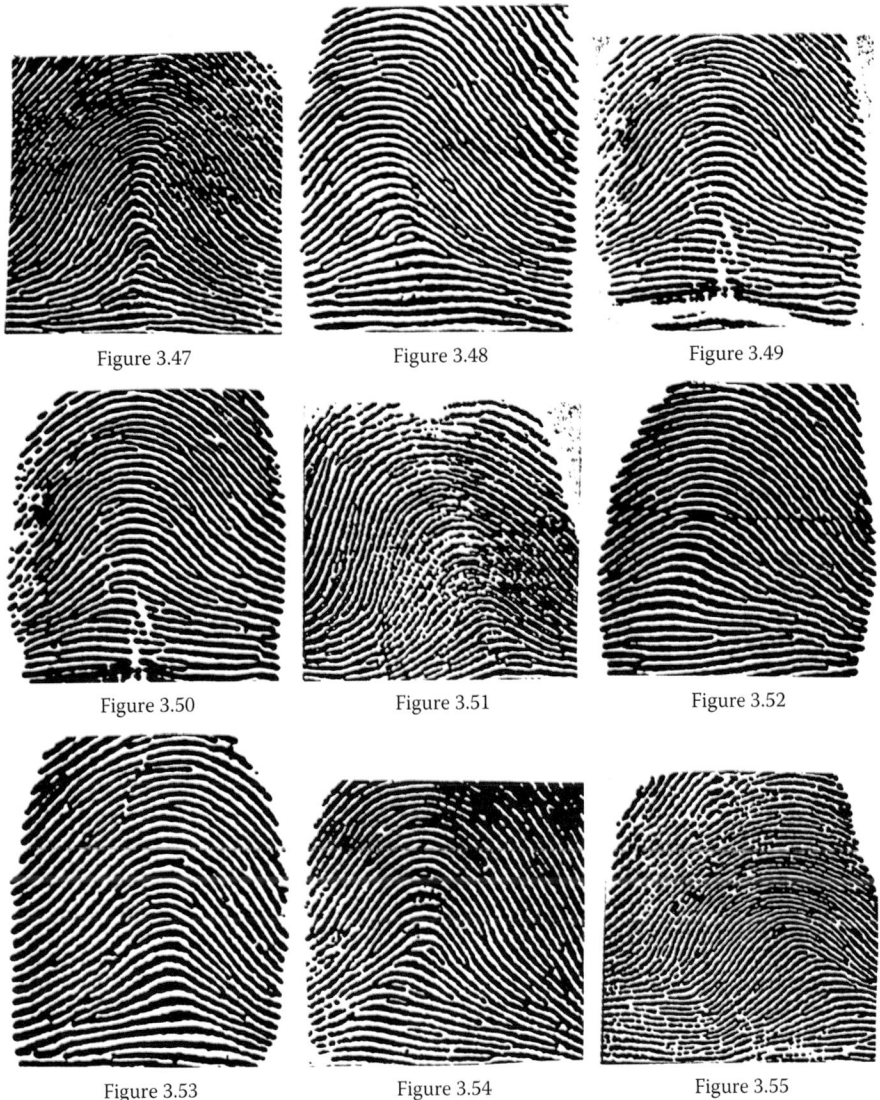

Figure 3.47

Figure 3.48

Figure 3.49

Figure 3.50

Figure 3.51

Figure 3.52

Figure 3.53

Figure 3.54

Figure 3.55

Figure 3.47–3.55 Plain arch patterns.

The Whorl Pattern

Definition: A whorl is that type of pattern in which at least two deltas are present with a *recurve* in front of each (Figures 3.56 through 3.103).

Types: The plain whorl, the central pocket loop whorl, the double loop whorl, and the accidental whorl.

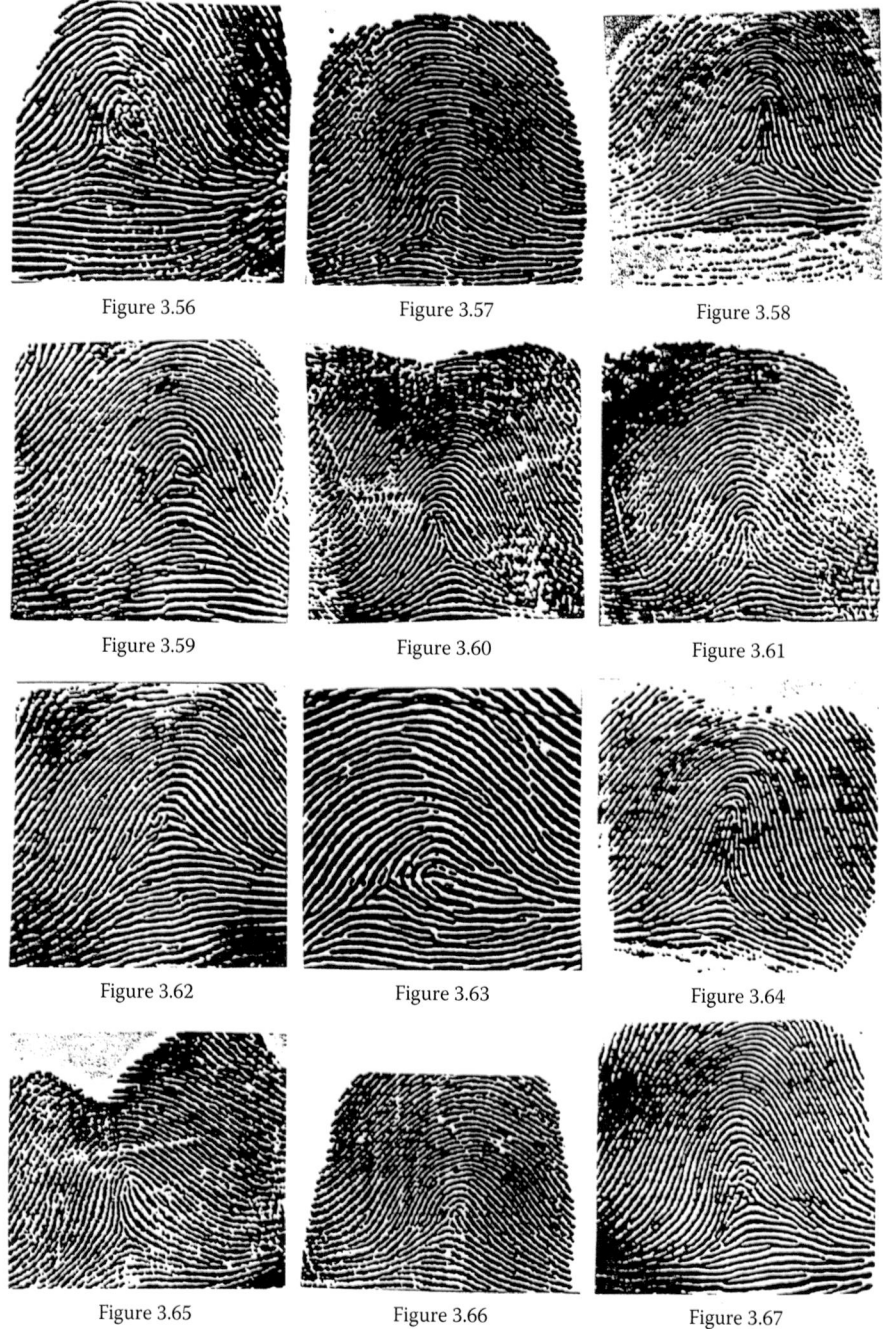

Figure 3.56

Figure 3.57

Figure 3.58

Figure 3.59

Figure 3.60

Figure 3.61

Figure 3.62

Figure 3.63

Figure 3.64

Figure 3.65

Figure 3.66

Figure 3.67

Figure 3.56–3.67 Tented arch patterns.

Fingerprint Pattern Types and Terminology

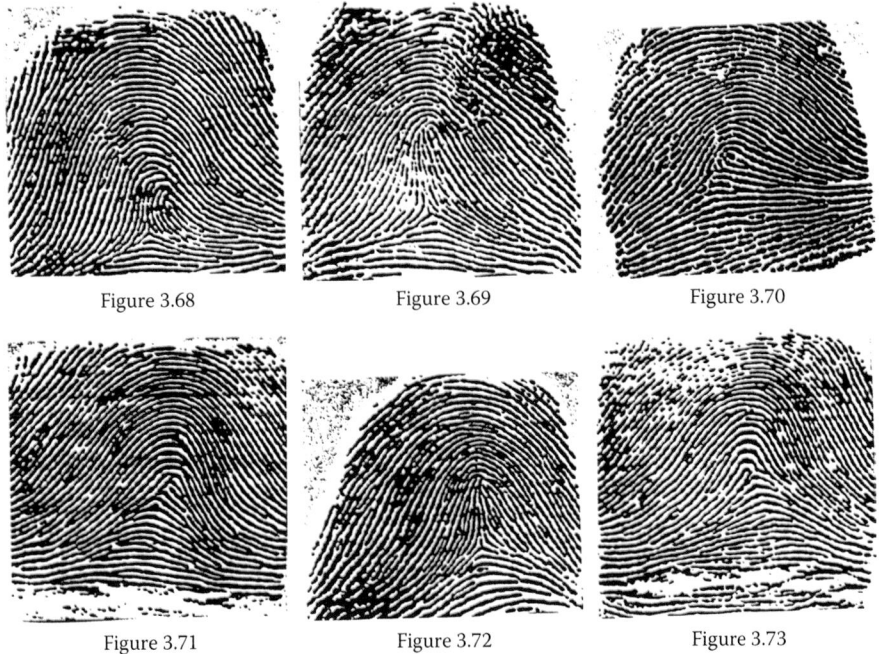

Figure 3.68 Figure 3.69 Figure 3.70

Figure 3.71 Figure 3.72 Figure 3.73

Figure 3.68–3.73 Tented arch patterns.

Plain Whorl

A plain whorl possesses two deltas and at least one ridge making a complete circuit, which may be spiral, oval, circular, or any variant of a circle (Figures 3.77 through 3.85).

Figure 3.74

Figure 3.75

1. The type lines for both deltas do not have to be the same ridge.
2. An imaginary line drawn between the two deltas *must* touch or cross at least one of the recurving ridges within the inner pattern (Figure 3.76).
3. A recurving ridge, however, which has an appendage connected with it, cannot be construed as a circuit as the recurve is spoiled (Figure 3.104).

Central Pocket Loop Whorl

Combines the features of both loops and whorls.

1. The pattern looks like a loop but has a small whorl inside the loop ridges.
2. It has two deltas, one at the edge of the pattern area, and one inside the pattern area just below the centermost ridges (inner delta).
3. It fulfills the requirements of the loop with one or more whorl ridges around the core.
4. This pattern is sometimes called a bulb or flower for obvious reasons (Figures 3.114–3.122).

Figure 3.76

Fingerprint Pattern Types and Terminology

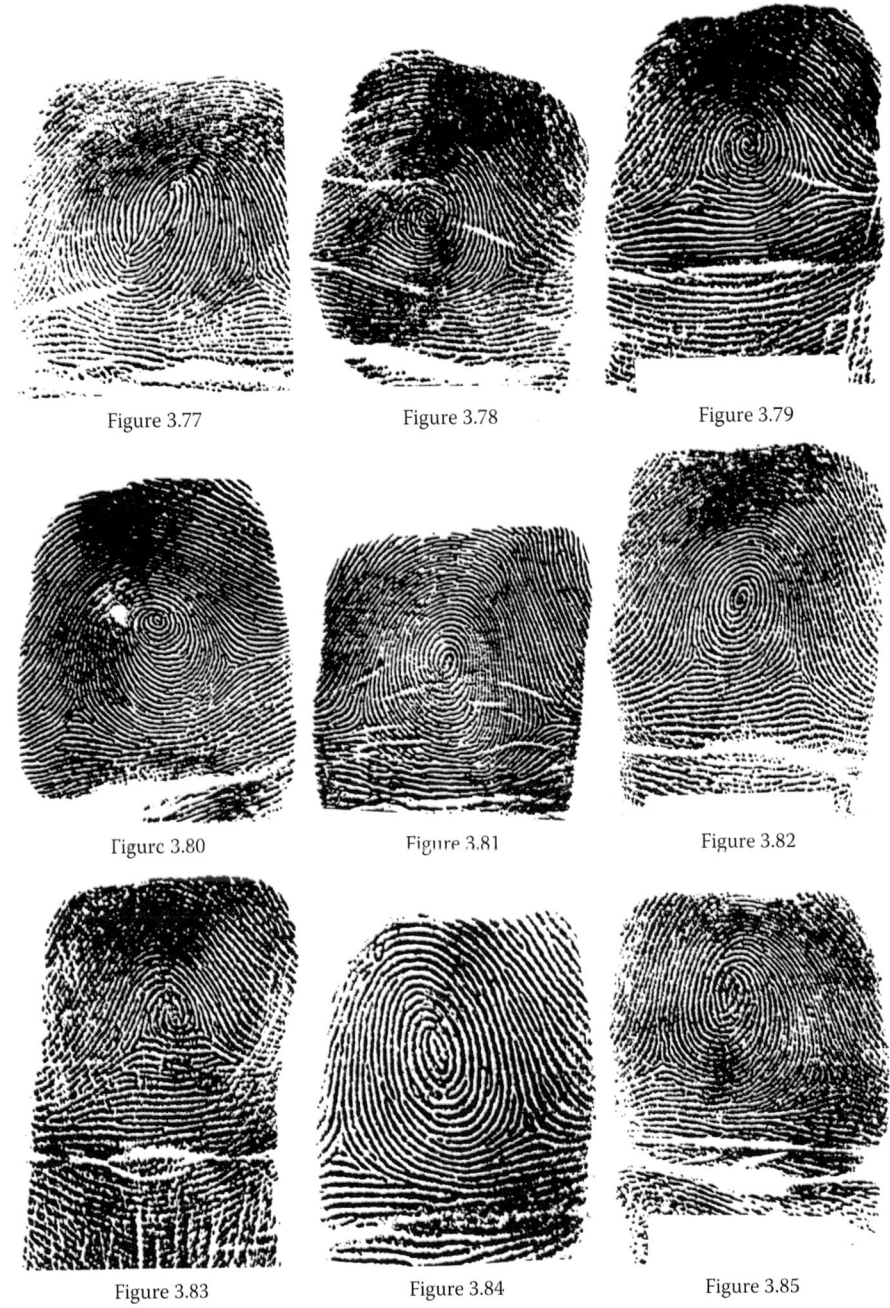

Figure 3.77

Figure 3.78

Figure 3.79

Figure 3.80

Figure 3.81

Figure 3.82

Figure 3.83

Figure 3.84

Figure 3.85

Figure 3.77–3.85 Plain whorl patterns.

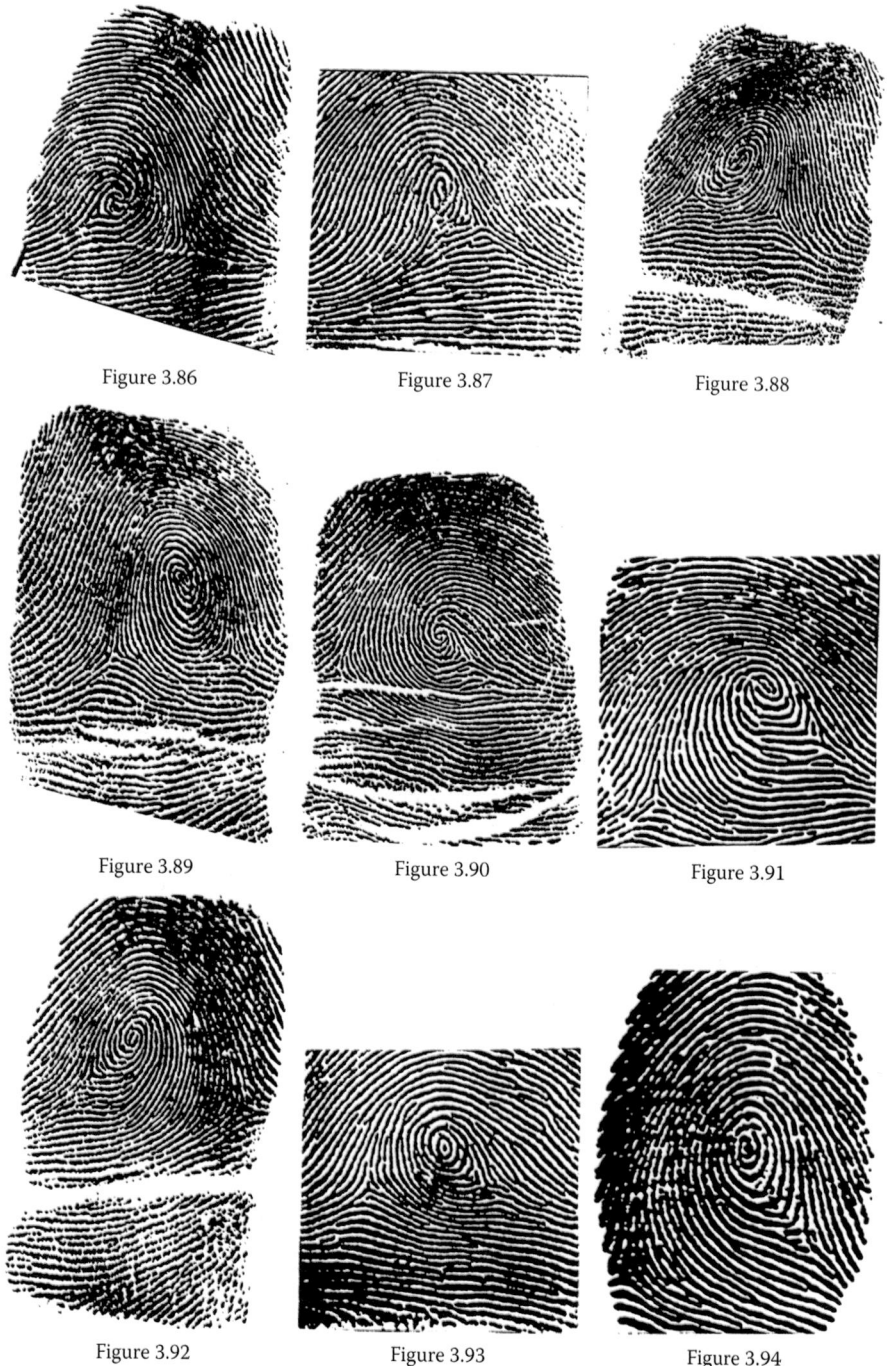

Figure 3.86 Figure 3.87 Figure 3.88
Figure 3.89 Figure 3.90 Figure 3.91
Figure 3.92 Figure 3.93 Figure 3.94

Figure 3.86–3.94 Central pocket loop whorl patterns.

Fingerprint Pattern Types and Terminology

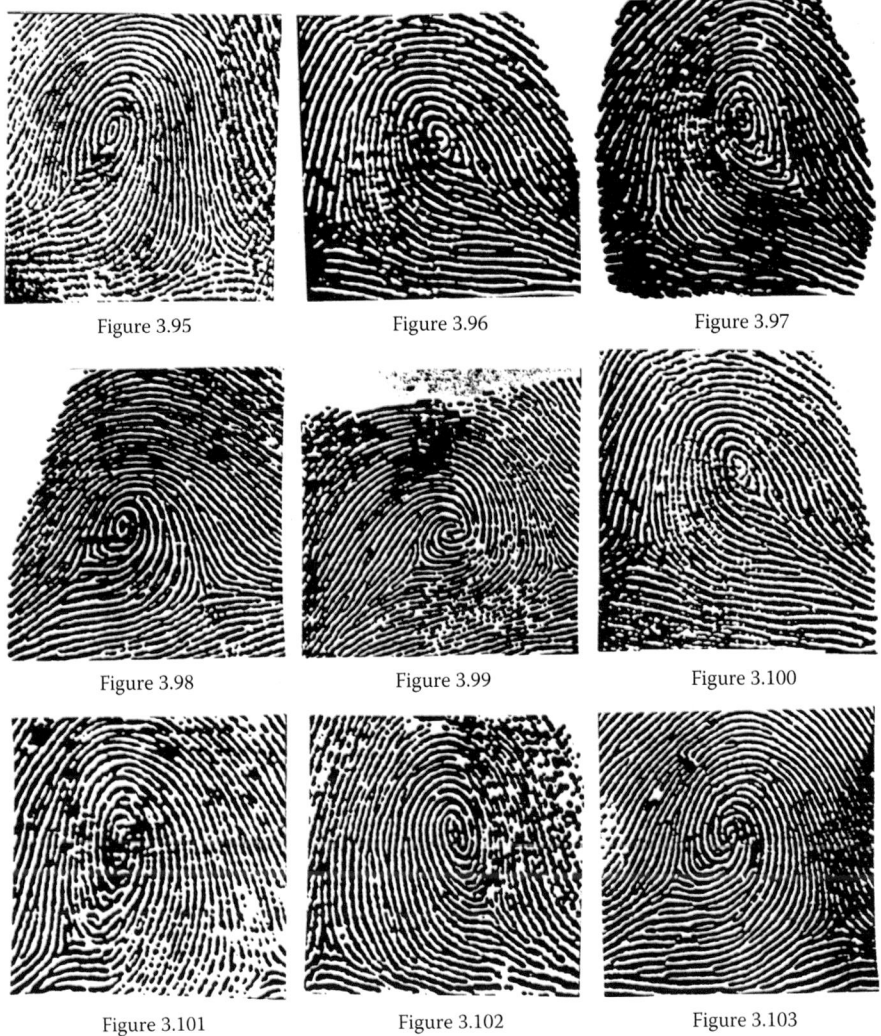

Figure 3.95 Figure 3.96 Figure 3.97
Figure 3.98 Figure 3.99 Figure 3.100
Figure 3.101 Figure 3.102 Figure 3.103

Figure 3.95–3.103 Central pocket loop whorl patterns.

Definition: The central pocket loop has two deltas and at least one ridge making a complete circuit, which may be spiral, oval, circular, or any variant of a circle (Figures 3.86 through 3.103).

1. One or more of the simple recurves of the loop type usually recurve a second time to form a pocket within the loop (inside delta).
2. This does not have to be a continuation of the first ridge or connected to it. Example: Loop convergence (Figure 3.123).

Figure 3.104

Figure 3.105 　　　　　Figure 3.106 　　　　　Figure 3.107

Figure 3.108 　　　　　Figure 3.109 　　　　　Figure 3.110

Figure 3.111 　　　　　Figure 3.112 　　　　　Figure 3.113

Figure 3.105–3.113 Double loop whorl patterns.

Fingerprint Pattern Types and Terminology

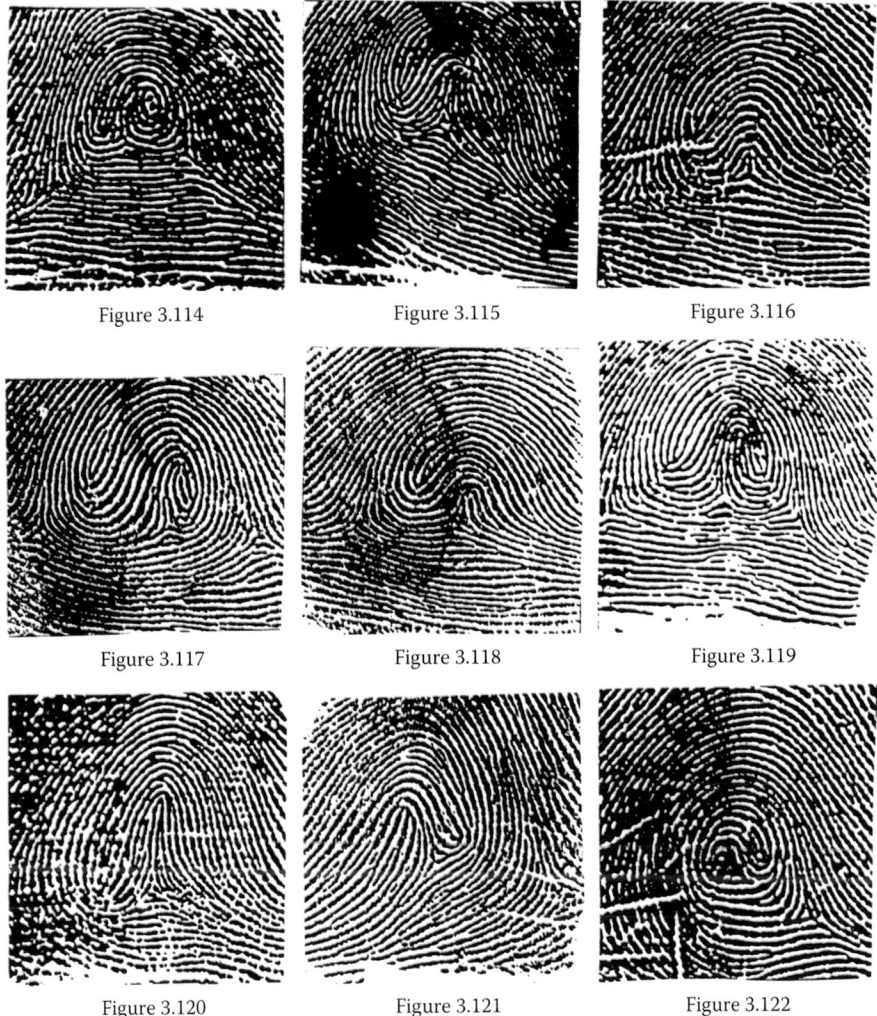

Figure 3.114

Figure 3.115

Figure 3.116

Figure 3.117

Figure 3.118

Figure 3.119

Figure 3.120

Figure 3.121

Figure 3.122

Figure 3.114–3.122 Accidental whorl patterns.

a. An imaginary line between the inner and outer delta *must not* touch or cross any of the recurving ridges within the inner pattern area (Figure 3.124).
b. In lieu of a recurve in front of the delta in the inner pattern area, an obstruction at right angles to the line of flow will suffice.
c. The obstruction may be curved or straight, connected or unattached to the recurve.
d. A dot cannot be considered an obstruction.

Figure 3.123

e. The inner line of flow is determined by drawing an imaginary line between the inner delta and the center of the innermost recurve or looping ridge (Figure 3.125).
f. A true recurving ridge does not have to cross the line of flow at right angles; an obstruction does.
g. If the recurve *or* obstruction has an appendage at the point of intersection of the line of flow, *at the delta side*, it is spoiled.

In a central pocket loop whorl, at least one recurve or obstruction at right angles to, free from appendage, must cross the inner line of flow (Figure 3.126).

Double Loop Whorl

A double loop whorl is a pattern that consists of two separate loop formations with two separate and distinct sets of shoulders and two deltas (2 × 2 × 2) (Figures 3.105 through 3.113).

Figure 3.124

Fingerprint Pattern Types and Terminology 51

Figure 3.125

Figure 3.126

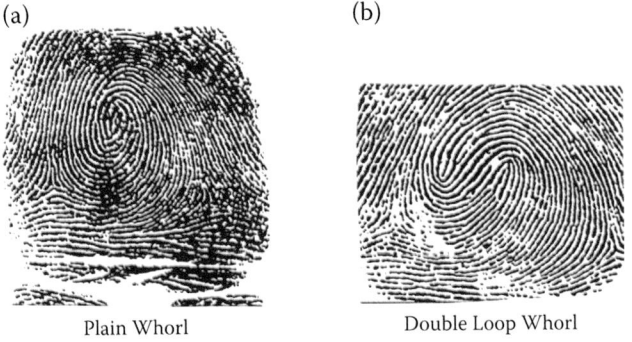

Figure 3.127

Figure 3.128

1. The loops may be connected by an appendaging ridge provided that it does not abut on the loop at right angles between the shoulders, spoiling it (Figure 3.127a and b).
2. The loops do not have to conform to the ridge count requirement of a plain loop (Figure 3.128).
3. It is not essential that both sides of a loop be of equal size or length (Figure 3.129).
4. It is not material from which side the loops enter. The loops may enter from either side or both from the same side.

Accidental Whorl

An accidental whorl is a pattern consisting of a combination of two different types of patterns, with the exception of the plain arch, with two or more deltas, or a pattern that possesses some of the requirements for two or more different types, or a pattern that conforms to none of the definitions (Figures 3.114 through 3.122).

Figure 3.129

Fingerprint Pattern Types and Terminology

Figure 3.130

Examples are as follows:

- Loop and Tented Arch (Note: The loop must appear over the tented arch. Where the loop does not appear in this position, the preferred pattern is a loop.)
- Loop and Plain Whorl (Figure 3.130)
- Loop and Central Pocket Loop (Figure 3.131)
- Combination of a Loop and Double Loop Whorl (Figure 3.132)

If there is an issue between two types of patterns in the whorl pattern or ridges that conform to more than one subdivision, the order of priority in preference is:

1. Accidental
2. Double loop
3. Central pocket loop
4. Plain

Figure 3.131

Figure 3.132

Ridge Tracing and Counting Whorl Patterns

1. Ridge tracing (For purposes of tracing, the extreme left delta and extreme right delta are of concern. Where there is a third delta, such as may be present in the center of the pattern, that delta is not counted; Figure 3.120.)
    a. Establish deltas.
    b. Starting at the left delta, trace ridges, moving outward away from the center of the pattern to where the ridge ends. Continue tracing until the point nearest or opposite the extreme right delta is reached.
    c. If the ridge bifurcates, the lower branch is followed.
    d. Examine other apparent ridge endings in the pattern to ensure that the ridge actually ends and is not caused by other factors such as improper inking, the presence of debris, and the like.
    e. The number of ridges between the tracing ridge and the right delta is counted.
    f. Values:
       Inner (I): Three or more ridges inside the right delta
       Meet (M): Fewer than three inside or outside right delta (0, 1, 2)
       Outer (O): Three or more ridges outside the right delta
    g. In accidental and double loop whorls, when the tracing passes inside of the right delta, stop at the nearest point to the right delta on the upward trend.
       Note: Whorl tracing will never begin on a type line.
2. Ridge counts in whorls:
    a. Used only in some extensions of classifications.

Fingerprint Pattern Types and Terminology

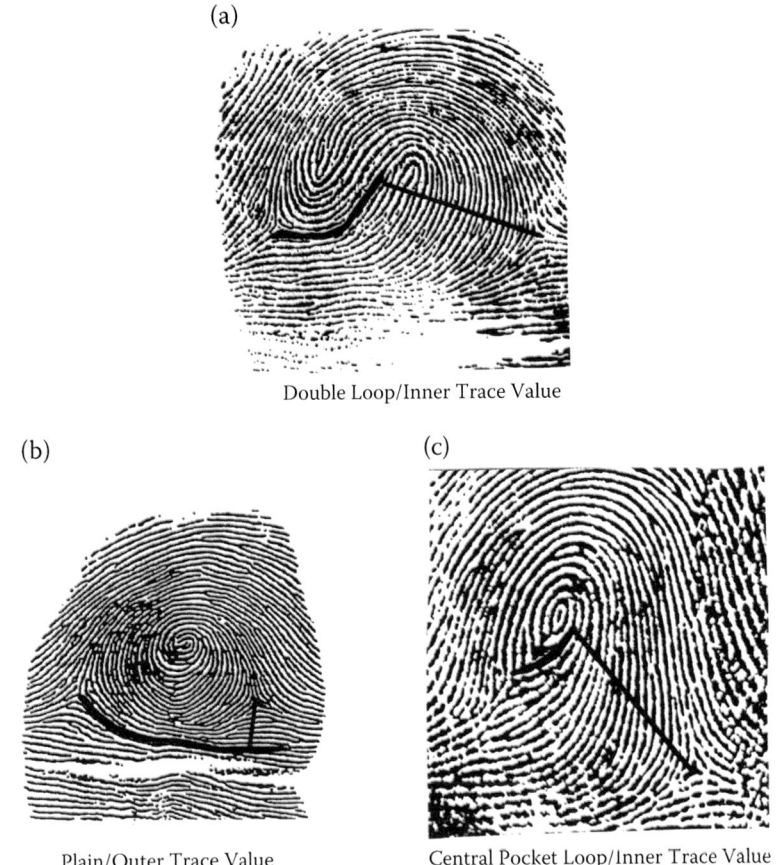

Figure 3.133 Whorl ridge tracing illustrations: (a) *Top*, double loop/inner trace value. (b) *Bottom left*, plain/outer trace value. (c) *Bottom right*, central pocket loop/inner trace value.

    b. Procedure:
        i. Count from the left delta to core on right hand.
        ii. Count from the right delta to core on left hand.
    c. If more than two deltas are present, use the one on the proper side and closest to the core (Figure 1.134).

The Palm Print

As with fingerprints, palms can be used for purposes of individualization, identification, and exclusion. Though not as many rules apply to the palm, the process whereby the palm is used for comparison, identification, and

Figure 3.134

individualization is the same. The palm is obviously labeled differently as a number of different palms possess a variety of creases and parts. The palm itself contains ridge characteristics such as deltas, bifurcations, and ending ridges but differs in the main parts. There are three primary divisions of the palm (Figure 3.135).

There are also various creases in the palm that are used for descriptive purposes (Figure 3.136).

- Interdigital
- Thenar
- Hypothenar

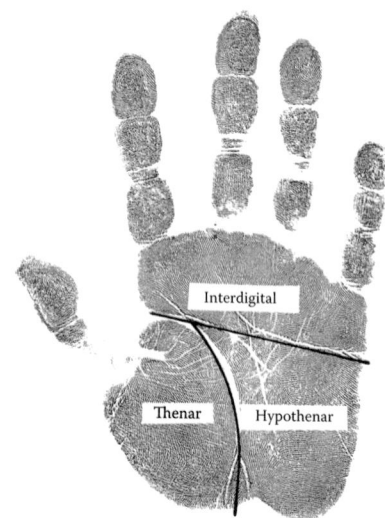

Figure 3.135 Divisions of the palm.

Fingerprint Pattern Types and Terminology

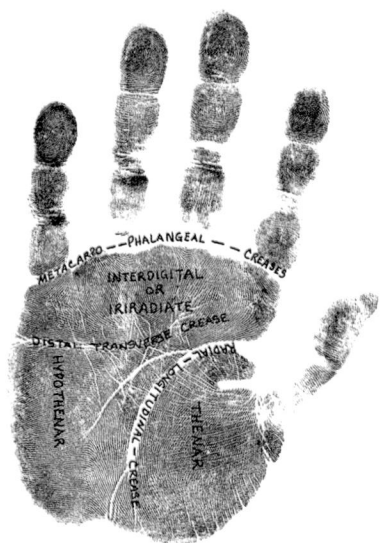

Figure 3.136 Creases in the palm.

Chapter 3 Study Questions

1. Define a loop pattern.
2. What are the essentials of a loop pattern?
3. What structures may be a delta?
4. What are the rules governing the choice between two deltas?
5. What are the shoulders of a loop?
6. What is meant by an appendage spoiling a loop?
7. Define the plain arch pattern.
8. What is the "crest" of an arch pattern?
9. What is another name for an arch pattern?
10. Will there be deltas, cores, recurves, or type lines in the plain arch pattern?
11. Define the tented arch pattern.
12. What are the three types of tented arches?
13. What is the test for an upthrust?
14. Can the converging of two ridges be considered to form a recurve?
15. What are the four types of whorl patterns?
16. What is the general definition applying to all whorl patterns?
17. What is the delta-to-delta test for a plain whorl?
18. What is the inner line of flow and how is it used?
19. Must both loops in a double loop whorl have a ridge count?
20. What type of pattern is formed by a combination of an arch and a loop?
21. What are the types of accidental whorl patterns?

Introduction to Classification Systems 4

As with any method of classification, the purpose of classifying fingerprints is to establish a set protocol to utilize for searching, filing, and comparison purposes. This protocol provides an orderly method with which to go from the general to the specific. As an example, how would one begin to search for a fingerprint pattern if that pattern has not been cataloged? Questions would certainly arise: What type of pattern are we trying to locate? Is the pattern a loop, whorl, or arch? Is there a specific flow to the pattern? If the pattern is a loop, is it a large or small count loop flowing to the left or to the right? If the pattern is a whorl, does it have an outer, inner, or meet trace value? Some of these basic questions give us direction to understand the need to have a method by which to search.

Henry with FBI Extension

One of the first, and certainly the most noted, of the classification systems was a system named after Sir Edward Henry. This identification system, when originally developed and implemented, consisted of four parts: primary, secondary, subsecondary, and final. The system has since undergone changes and now includes an FBI (U.S. Federal Bureau of Investigation) extension, which changes the original configuration from four to six categories. There is a seventh category, if a second subsecondary is used. Since the introduction of technology and various automated fingerprint identification (AFIS) systems, this method has come to be known as the manual method. In later parts of the book, AFIS systems are discussed.

As with any process that is newly introduced, with the *Henry system of classification* being no exception, the need to practice and understand the system is tantamount. The current components of the Henry system are:

1. *Key:* The ridge count of the first loop appearing on the card, excluding little fingers.
2. *Major:* The ridge count or trace value of the thumbs.
3. *Primary:* The numeric value of each finger containing a whorl pattern.
4. *Secondary:* A capital letter indicating the pattern of index fingers.
5. *Subsecondary:* Values of counts and traces of loops and whorls of the index, middle, and ring fingers.
6. *Final:* Ridge count of loops appearing on little fingers.

An example of the form of the Henry classification is shown in the following:

Key	Major	Primary	Secondary	Subsecondary	Final
4	O	5	U	IOI	10
	I	17	U	IOI	

Where does the information for classification come from? The fingerprint card gives us the necessary information. Knowing how to read and insert appropriate information onto the fingerprint card is important. The process of inserting information onto the card is known as *blocking the card*. Figures 4.1–4.3 show examples of fingerprint cards.

Blocking the card consists of *inserting the appropriate information, consisting of numbers, letters, and symbols in the appropriate places on the card*. Below is an example of the layout and position of the fingers on the fingerprint card.

1—Rt. Thumb	2—Rt. Index	3—Rt. Middle	4—Rt. Ring	5—Rt. Little
6—Lt. Thumb	7—Lt. Index	8—Lt. Middle	9—Lt. Ring	10—Lt. Little
Left four fingers—flats Simultaneous laydowns		Lt. Thumb	Rt. Thumb	Rt. Four fingers—flats Simultaneous laydowns

Based on the fingerprints and their interpretation, the following information should be placed on the card in the appropriate places.

1. **Index fingers**—A, T, R, W, U as decided by the interpretation. Placed under the index fingerprint. Note: A = arch, T = tented arch, R = radial loop, W = whorl, U = ulnar loop (\ /).
2. **Other fingers**—Small letters as appropriate (i.e., a, t, r). Placed under all fingerprints except index fingerprints.
3. **Ulnar loops**—Diagonal slash in the direction of flow.
4. **Whorls**—W where appropriate.
5. **Counts or traces**—In the upper right corner of the box.

Introduction to Classification Systems

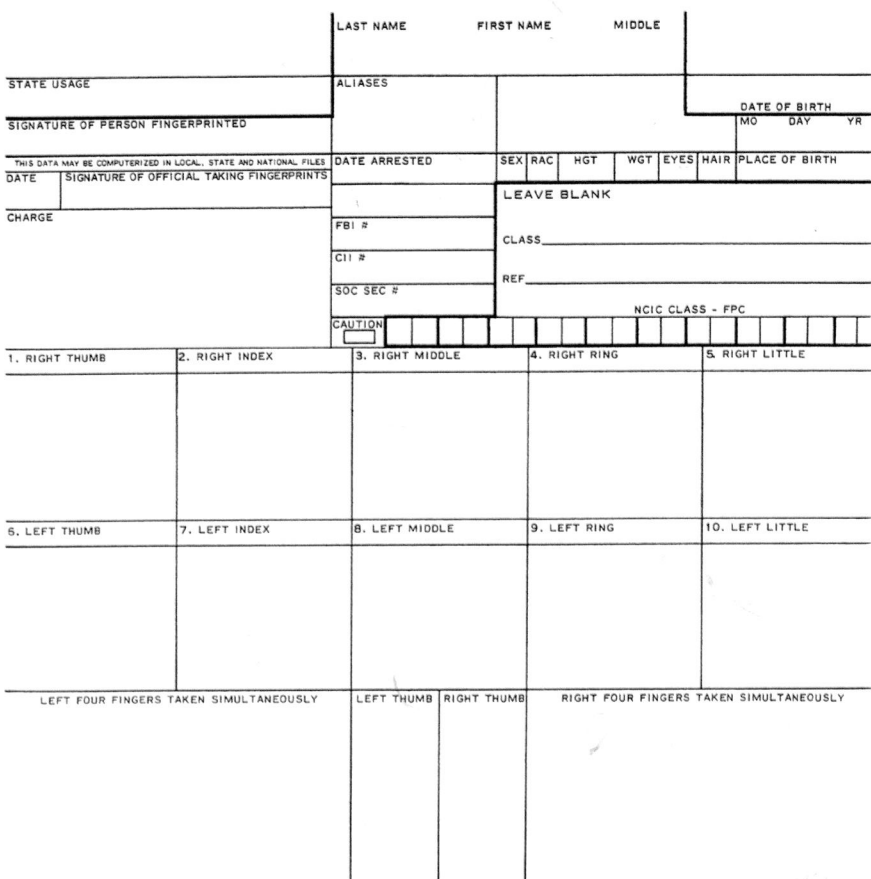

Figure 4.1 Fingerprint card (tenprint).

6. Reference if necessary (giving an alternative).

It should be noted that the right thumb is always finger number 1, and the left little finger is finger number 10. Also note that fingers that oppose are opposite to each other on the card, for example, 1/6, 2/7, 3/8, 4/9, 5/10.

For the purposes of the classification, the right hand and even number fingers go above the line. The left hand and odd number fingers go below the line.

To begin the process of manual classification, one starts with the *Primary*. Remember, *Primary* is the numeric value of the finger where a whorl appears. Any type of whorl is assigned a value. Ridge tracing does not enter into the primary classification. The numeric value was established with the advent of the Henry system. Whatever finger the whorl appears on,

Figure 4.2 Fingerprint card (left hand).

that finger assumes that value of the square. Upon adding up the numbers, always add 1 to the value (the numeric chart appears below). Even number fingers, 2, 4, 6, 8, and 10, are registered above (numerator) the classification line. Odd number fingers 1, 3, 5, 7, and 9, are registered below (denominator) the line.

(1)	(2)	(3)	(4)	(5)
16	16	8	8	4
4	2	2	1	1
(6)	(7)	(8)	(9)	(10)

Introduction to Classification Systems

Figure 4.3 Fingerprint card (right hand).

As an example of how the primary is completed, look at the card below. Whorls appear on fingers 2, 8, and 10. The value would be 16 + 2 + 1 = 19 + 1 for a primary value of 20, which would go above the line (numerator), as those are even number fingers. Whorls also appear in fingers 3, 5, and 7. The value would be 8 + 4 + 2 = 14 + 1 for a primary of 15, which would go below the line (denominator), as those are odd number fingers.

(1)	(2)	(3)	(4)	(5)
	W	W		W
	W	W		W
(6)	(7)	(8)	(9)	(10)

Primary
20
15

There are 1,024 different combinations of whorl values. Where all whorls appear on the card, the primary classification will be 32 over 32. Where no whorls appear on the card, the primary classification will be 1 over 1.

The *Secondary* portion of the classification indicates the pattern type of the index fingers and is always indicated by a capital letter.

- A = Arch
- T = Tented arch
- R = Radial loop
- W = Whorl
- U = Ulnar loop

The designation of the capital letters will always be right hand over left hand on the classification line. The *secondary* portion of the classification will be indicated by placing the information immediately to the right of the primary classification. See the example below.

Primary	Secondary
17	W
2	U

There is also a *secondary, small letter grouping*. Some say the small letter grouping is part of the subsecondary. In any event, whenever there is a small letter grouping in the classification, the secondary and subsecondary become one in the same. Let us first look at the small letter groupings. Whenever an arch, tented arch, or radial loop appears in other than the index fingerprints, those patterns are indicated by a small letter:

A = a   T = t   R = r

The small letter groups should appear next to the capital letter of the secondary in the sequence in which they occur. For example, if the fingerprint of an index finger is a whorl, and that of the middle finger is a tented arch, the small t would then be placed to the immediate right of the whorl in order of its appearance on the card. If the thumb were an arch, for example, the small letter indicator would then appear to the immediate left of the index finger. In the secondary classification, the index finger can be seen as the anchor and all small letter group patterns appear to the right or left of the index finger (see the example below).

Introduction to Classification Systems

Primary	Secondary
18	Wt
1	

	W	T		
				W

When other patterns appear on the card along with the small letter groups, (U, W) they are indicated by a hyphen (-).

When two or more of the small letters occur next to each other, they are indicated by a number with the letters (see the examples below).

Primary	Secondary
1	U-t
3	rW

Primary	Secondary
1	U2t
1	tU-a

		U	U	T	
R	W				W

		U	T	T	
T	U	U	A		

Where there is a small letter group in the secondary, the subsecondary and major divisions are dispensed with. It should also be noted that approximately 7 to 10 percent of all patterns are small letter types.

Small letter groups can lend themselves to confusion. Remember, the small letter groups are indicated in the classification where they appear on the card with the index finger as the anchor indicated by a capital letter.

The *Subsecondary* division of the classification is the grouping of ridge count and/or whorl trace symbols for the index, middle, and ring fingerprints appearing on the card. For classification purposes, the right hand is indicated above the line, the left hand is indicated below the line. The subsecondary division appears to the immediate right of the secondary division on the card. The subsecondary is indicated by a letter.

To determine which symbol will be used to indicate the ridge count for a loop pattern, a conversion of ridge counts into a letter must be done and that letter placed onto the classification. The conversion chart is:

Ridge Count Conversion

Index finger:	01 to 09 inner (I);	10+ outer (O)
Middle finger:	01 to 10 inner (I):	11+ outer (O)
Ring finger:	01 to 13 inner (I):	14+ outer (O)

Conversion Chart for Ridge Counts

Index	Middle	Ring
1 to 9 inner (I)	1 to 13 inner (I)	1 to 10 inner (I)
10+ outer (O)	14+ outer (O)	11+ outer (O)
1 to 10 inner (I)	1 to 9 inner (I)	1 to 13 inner (I)
11+ outer (O)	10+ outer (O)	14+ outer (O)
Index	Middle	Ring

Whorl ridge tracings are indicated by the value of the tracing:

(I) = Inner—3 or more ridges inside the right delta
(M) = Meet—0, 1, or 2 ridges inside or outside the right delta
(O) = Outer— 3 or more ridges outside the right delta

An example of how the conversion appears from the fingerprint card to the classification is:

Primary	Secondary	Subsecondary
24	W	OOO
I	U	OMO

11 U \	O W \	14 U \	16 U \	8 U \
I W	15 U /	M W	14 U /	I W

Introduction to Classification Systems

Note: There is an additional division that may be utilized to further subdivide the fingerprint classification. The further subdivision is called the *second subsecondary*. This division has rarely been used for classification purposes. However, the division does exist and bears mentioning. As with the secondary, the second subsecondary has a conversion chart that differs from the subsecondary. Rather than burden the reader with additional information, I feel it only necessary to mention the division as an ancillary part of the classification system.

The *Major* division of the classification consists of the ridge count or ridge trace value of the thumbs, right hand over left hand. The designation on the card appears immediately to the left of the primary. (If there is an **A** or **T** in the thumbs, there will be no major classification. Remember if there is a small letter group in the secondary, the subsecondary and major are also dispensed with.)

Whorl trace values will be indicated by inner **(I)**, meet **(M)**, or outer **(O)**.

Loop counts must be converted into small **(S)**, medium **(M)**, or large **(L)**.

When deciding which value to assign the thumbs for a loop conversion, *always count the left thumb first*. Based on the ridge count of the left thumbprint, the right thumb designation can be determined based on the conversion chart.

- Left thumb conversion for ridge counts:
  - 1 to 11 small (S), 12 to 16 medium (M), 17+ large (L)
- Right thumb:
  - If the ridge count of the left thumb is 16 or less, the same conversion is used for the left and right thumbs
  - If the ridge count of the left thumb is 17 or more, a larger conversion chart must be utilized: 1 to 17 small (S), 18 to 22 medium (M), 23+ large (L)

Where a whorl appears in the left thumbprint, the right thumb is converted as though the left thumb had a ridge count of smaller than 17. In other words, use the smaller conversion chart to apply to the right thumb.

To better understand the conversion process, the chart shown below indicates the conversions for the subsecondary and the major.

Where left thumb is 16 or fewer	Right	Hand	
01 to 11 S 12 to 16 M 17 + L	01 to 09 I 10 + O	01 to 10 I 11 + O	01 to 13 I 14 + O
Where left thumb is 17 or more 01 to 17 S 18 to 22 M 23 + L			
01 to 11 S 12 to 16 M 17 + L	Left 01 to 09 I 10 + O	Hand 01 to 10 I 11 + O	01 to 13 I 14 + O

An example of the proper placement and conversion of the fingerprints into their respective places in the classification is shown below.

The remaining two divisions of the classification are the easiest to understand as there are no conversions to undergo. One simply observes the pattern and the ridge count and expresses that in the classification. As you may have noticed, both refer to ridge counts, which means the remaining divisions consist of loop patterns. If there are no loop patterns on the card, neither of these divisions will be noted. The divisions are the *key* and the *final*.

Major	Primary	Secondary	Subsecondary
M	19	W	MOI
L	6	U	IMO

(1)	(2)	(3)	(4)	(5)
18 U \	M W	11 U \	12 U \	O W
17 U /	06 U /	M W	O W	12 U /
(6)	(7)	(8)	(9)	(10)

Introduction to Classification Systems

The *Final* consists of the ridge count of a loop appearing in the fingerprints of little fingers. In order of preference, the right little finger is examined first to see if there is a loop pattern. If there is no loop pattern in the right little finger, then the left little finger is examined. If neither the prints from the right nor the left little fingers possess a loop, there will be no final.

The *final* division may be placed above (numerator) the classification line if the loop appears in the right little finger. If the loop appears in the left little finger, the ridge count will be placed below (denominator) the classification line. The final cannot consist of both fingers; the final will consist of one or the other.

In large whorl sections, whorls can also be counted, but this is rare. However, if a whorl is chosen to be included, there are rules that must be adhered to. The following rules apply when using whorls as the final.

- If the whorl appears on the right hand, one counts from the left delta to the core.
- If the whorl appears on the left hand, one counts from the right delta to the core.
- If there are two cores, count from the delta to the core which is the fewest number of ridges away.
- If the pattern is a double loop, count from the delta to the core of the upright loop.
- If loops are horizontal, use the one nearest core.

The *key* consists of the count of the first loop appearing on the card excluding the little fingers. The little fingers are reserved for inclusion in the final. The designation for the key is always indicated above the line farthest to the left on the classification.

Below is an example of a fingerprint card and a complete classification of all the divisions of the modified Henry system with the FBI extension.

Key	Major	Primary	Secondary	Subsecondary	Final
9	O	9	U	IOM	
	L	22	U	OOO	10

O	9	12	M	I
W	U	U	W	W
17	12	14	O	10
U	U	U	W	U
/	/	/	/	/

What happens if the prints one is taking are not clear and legible? What happens if the pattern cannot be determined or if there are temporary or permanent injuries to the person being fingerprinted. How does one deal with these issues? How does one classify these types of fingerprints? As with other aspects of the Henry system, provisions have been made for just such occasions. The following information addresses special issues related to fingerprints.

- Classification of Scarred Patterns
    - When the following cannot be determined_____Give
        a. Pattern type and value_____Class of opposite finger
        b. Pattern only_____ Pattern of opposite finger with actual value and reference
        c. Count or Trace value_____Probable with reference
        d. Opposite fingers scarred_____Meet whorls
- Classification of Amputated Fingers
    - Missing fingers____Class
        a. One_____Same as opposite with all references
        b. Two or more_____Same as opposite with no references
        c. Opposite_____Meet whorls
    - Fingers missing at birth are treated as amputations
    - If all ten fingers are missing_____ $\frac{M32WMMM}{M32WMMM}$ (meet whorls)
- If both hands are amputated, take footprints.
    - FBI maintains footprint files.
- If there is a partially amputated tip, it is classed as it appears and is referenced to the opposite finger.
- Classification of Bandaged and Unprintable Fingers
    - One lacking—All references—opposite fingers.
    - Two or more—Opposite class with no references.
    - Opposites—Meet whorls.
    - If a pattern can be seen, it can be described.
        "Ulnar loop of about 9 ridge count."
- Make all possible attempts to print the individual when the injury is healed.

Referencing

What is referencing? Referencing is an alternate choice that is displayed on the classification to indicate that although the classification may be indicated a certain way, it may also be something else. For example, a pattern

Introduction to Classification Systems

may be indicated as a loop with a ridge count of three, but the pattern may also be a tented arch. Or one may not be certain of a ridge count or trace value. What does referencing typically look like?

Class	9	M	9	U	IOM	
		L	22	U	OOO	10
Ref	8				MMO	
						11

- Always reference patterns questionable in interpretation, type, ridge count, or trace value.
- Factors making referencing necessary:
  - Variation in individual judgment and eyesight
  - The amount of ink and/or pressure used
  - Differences in the width of the rolled impression
  - Worn ridges caused by disease, age, or occupation
  - Amputations, temporary or permanent scars, and bandaged fingers
  - Crippled hands

For the highest degree of accuracy, compare all rolled impressions with the flat impressions. This will also give a sequence of patterns. All ridge count and traces that are "line counts" should be searched in both sections. When in doubt, assign the preferred class and place the reference class under it.

Filing Sequence

Due to technology and a variety of other factors, manual filing and searching is a rarity these days. However, the Henry filing system needs to be discussed in order to understand how the system is and was utilized, and how fingerprints were filed and searched. When the filing process is done, the fingerprints are filed the same way they are classed, m by division.

    A. *Primary*—The prints are filed according to their numeric designation. For example, 1/1 through 1/32 would first be searched. Then 2/1 through 2/32 and so on, until the search concludes with 32/32. The denominator remains constant until the numerator is exhausted.

    B. *Secondary*—The index fingers are searched.

        1. Capital letter of index fingers.

            a. A/A through W/W. In order of preference A/A, A/T, A/R,

A/U, A/W. Continue through the search, until concluding with W/W.
   2. Small letter sequencing.
      a. Denominator preferred.
         i. Count of small letters (lesser preceding greater)
         ii. Position of letters (left preceding right)
         iii. Type of letters, a, t, r.
C. *Subsecondary*—Ridge count or trace value indicated by a letter of the index, middle, and ring fingers.
   1. III/III though OOO/OOO
   2. Denominator remains constant until the numerator is exhausted.
D. *Major*—Ridge counts or trace values of the thumbs.
   1. Loops in thumbs: S/S to L/L
   2. Whorls in thumbs: I/I to O/O
   3. Whorl in the right thumb, loop in the left thumb: I/S to O/L
   4. Loop in the right thumb, whorl in the left thumb: S/I to L/O
E. *Final*—Ridge count of loop appearing in the little fingers.
   1. Numeric sequence from one out.
F. *Key*—First loop appearing on the card excluding little fingers.
   1. Numeric sequence from one out.

NCIC Classification System

The acronym NCIC stands for National Crime Information Center, which is a computerized system based in Washington, DC. This system is a computer database of wanted persons. The classification process used with this method is much easier to understand than is the Henry system as there are fewer rules to follow. However, the system is based on the Henry system. The system uses twenty characters on a line. This means each finger will be represented by two characters. The characters are representative of patterns and subgroup symbols. There are four categories to this system that are considered for inclusion. The groups are Arches, Whorls, Loops, and Others.

Introduction to Classification Systems

Pattern	Character
A. Arches	
1. Plain	AA
2. Tented	TT
B. Whorls—A ridge trace value must also be included in the characters.	
I = Inner M = Meet O = Outer	
1. Plain	PI, PM, PO
2. Central Pocket Loop Whorl	CI, CM, CO
3. Double Loop Whorl	DI, DM, DO
4. Accidental	XI, XM, XO
C. Loops—Must have two digits. If the number is lower than 10, a 0 must be placed in front of the number.	
1. Ulnar loop	Actual ridge count: 1–9 = 01 – 09
2. Radial loop	Actual ridge count + 50
D. Other	
1. Missing/Amputated	XX
2. Scarred	SR
Example:	
I 9 I 12 14	
W U CP U U	PI09CI121462AAPMDMTT
12 M M	
R A W DL T	

IAFIS

Recent changes in the designations of fingerprints by the FBI within the NCIC system, as a result of new Integrated Automated Fingerprint Identification System (IAFIS) designations, are based on fingerprint patterns. The new NCIC classification system will eventually replace the Henry Classification, as well as the old NCIC code system. The new IAFIS NCIC system will still require two characters per finger or a total of twenty characters on a line.

Both the old and the new codes are indicated below for clarity of information.

	Old: NCIC	New: IAFIS
Plain arch	AA	AU
Tented arch	TT	AU
Ulnar loop (right hand)	Actual Ridge Count	RS (right slant)
Ulnar loop (left hand)	Actual Ridge Count	LS (left slant)

(continued)

	Old: NCIC	New: IAFIS
Radial loop (right hand)	Actual Ridge Count + 50	LS (left slant)
Radial loop (left hand)	Actual Ridge Count + 50	RS (right slant)
Plain whorl (inner trace value)	PI	WU
Plain whorl (meet trace value)	PM	WU
Plain whorl (outer trace value)	PO	WU
Central pocket loop (inner trace value)	CI	WU
Central pocket loop (meet trace value)	CM	WU
Central pocket loop (outer trace value)	CO	WU
Double loop whorl (inner trace value)	DI	WU
Double loop whorl (meet trace value)	DM	WU
Double loop whorl (outer trace value)	DO	WU
Accidental whorl (inner trace value)	XI	WU
Accidental whorl (meet trace value)	XM	WU
Accidental whorl (outer trace value)	XO	WU
Scarred	SR	SR
Amputated	XX	XX
Where a print or pattern cannot be classified	UC	UC
Where a print is unattainable	UP	UP

To further clarify the application of the new IAFIS designation on the NCIC inquiry, the following example shows the fingerprint class (old) with the pattern class (new).

Fingerprint Class (NCIC)	Pattern Class (IAFIS)
PO CO PM 15 11 PO DO 12 14 08	WU WU WU RS RS WU WU LS LS LS

Other Fingerprint Systems (Manual Methods or Systems)

1. The single finger system, which is also known as the Battley system, was developed by Chief Inspector Henry Battley of the New York State fingerprint bureau.
2. The single hand system was patterned after a system developed by Anita Field of the Los Angeles Police department.
3. San Francisco Police Department Five Finger system.

It should also be noted that a variety of other systems have been developed and implemented throughout the world. However, with the advent of AFIS or IAFIS, many of the manual systems that have been developed are no longer being used.

The Automated Fingerprint Identification System (AFIS) is a computerized designation of fingerprint patterns for searching within the database. Designation using this system is the least complicated method. This method is based on pattern recognition. There are five possible designations that may be used for classification purposes: A, W, R, L, S.

- A = Arch or tented arch patterns
- W = Any type of whorl (plain, double loop, central pocket, accidental)
- R = Right slanted loop (for purposes of AFIS, it does not matter if the loop is an ulnar or radial loop, only that the flow is to the right).
- L = Left slanted loop (for purposes of AFIS, it do not matter if the loop is an ulnar or radial loop, only that the flow is to the left). As a reminder, to determine the line of flow, begin at the core and follow the ridges away from the core to determine the flow of the pattern.
- S = Scar (this designation is where a pattern cannot be determined or the damage to the pattern is severe).
- X = Amputated or missing finger.

Chapter 4 Study Questions

1. What is the purpose of the fingerprint classification system?
2. What do we mean by "blocking" the fingerprint card?
3. How is the primary obtained and determined?
4. Why was it necessary to add extensions to the Henry system?
5. What is done when a finger or fingers are bandaged?
6. In determining the major classification, why is it so important to count or view the left thumb first?
7. How is the secondary determined?
8. What is the key?
9. Explain the small letter group in the subsecondary.
10. What is the NCIC?
11. Describe the NCIC system giving appropriate symbols.
12. How many fingerprint types are there in the IAFIS system?
13. Name the fingerprint types in IAFIS.
14. What is the NCIC designation of a missing finger?
15. What is the NCIC designation of a scarred finger?
16. What do we do when both hands are amputated?
17. In the NCIC system, how is a radial loop indicated?
18. How would an accidental whorl be indicated in the NCIC system?

Part II

Development, Identification, and Presentation of Fingerprints

5

Known/Direct/Inked Fingerprints: Processing Techniques for Unknown/Latent Fingerprints

Known Fingerprints

Whether the method of taking inked prints is manual or through the use of a live scan, the process of obtaining good quality prints is basically the same. Taking a good quality fingerprint from a known source that can be used at a later time for a variety of purposes, from searching to individualization, is the ultimate goal. The terms *known*, *direct*, and *inked* are considered synonymous. Simply stated, these are prints taken from a known source. The clarity of the prints should be sufficient to allow for the comparison process to be conducted. These prints may also be known as tenprint cards.

Manual Method

I. Equipment required for taking known fingerprints (Figure 5.1)
    A. *Inking Plate*: Hard, rigid, scratch-resistant surface; glass, metal, or scratch-resistant plastic
        1. The inking plate should be affixed to a wood or other solid frame to prevent breakage.
        2. The inking plate should be elevated to a height to allow the subject's arm/hand to assume a horizontal position.

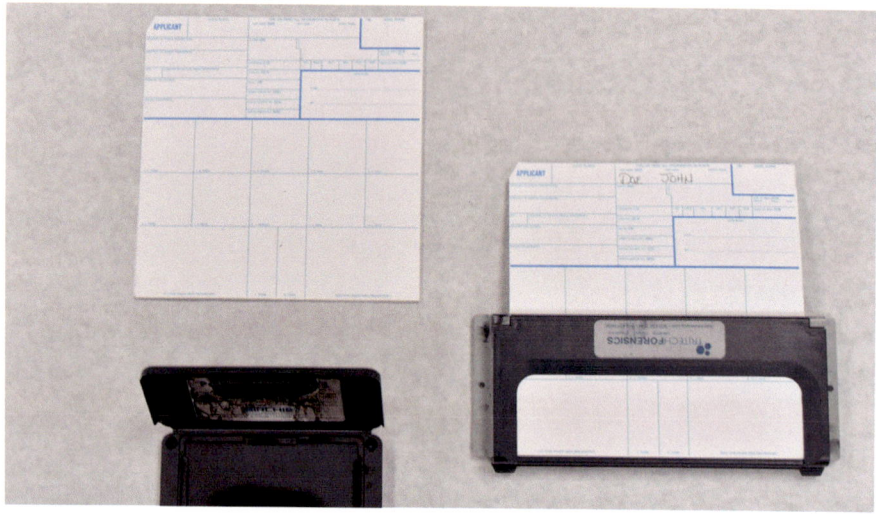

Figure 5.1 Manual fingerprint equipment.

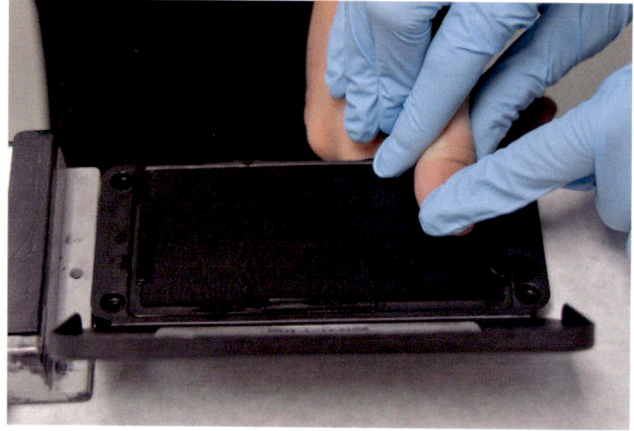

Figure 5.2 Manual fingerprint methodology.

    B. *Cardholder*: Used to hold the card flat and maintain an appropriate surface for registering required fingerprint information.

    C. *Printer's Ink*: Required to provide the necessary transfer medium to obtain proper finger and/or palm prints. Printer's ink is used due to its quick-drying properties, ease of use, and permanence.

Known/Direct/Inked Fingerprints 81

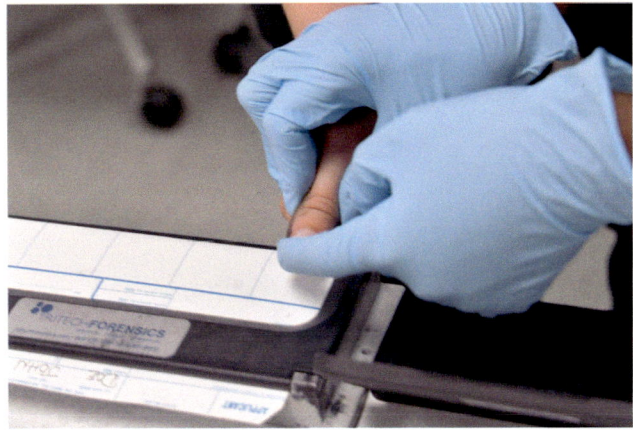

Figure 5.3 Manual fingerprint technique (rolling prints).

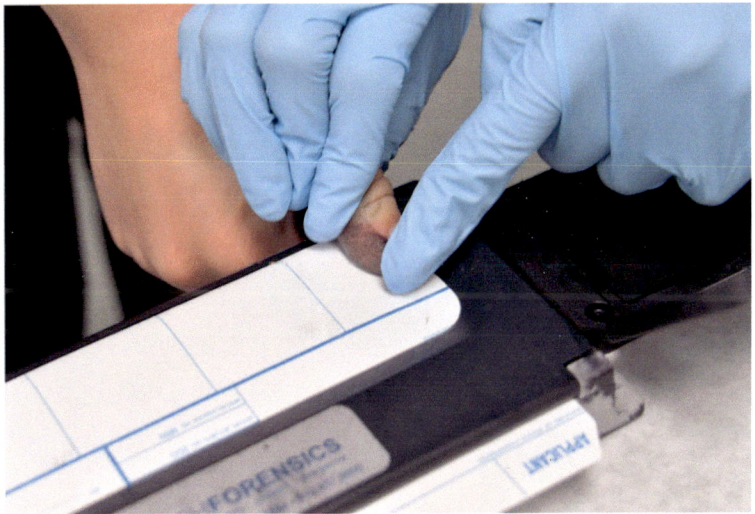

Figure 5.4 Manual fingerprint technique (rolling prints).

D. *Roller*: Preferably 6 inches long by 2 inches in diameter. Used to provide a uniform layer of ink onto the inking plate. The ink film must be sufficient to provide a transfer medium, but not too much to prevent proper inking of fingerprints.
E. *Fingerprint Card*: Standard 8 × 8 inch identification card

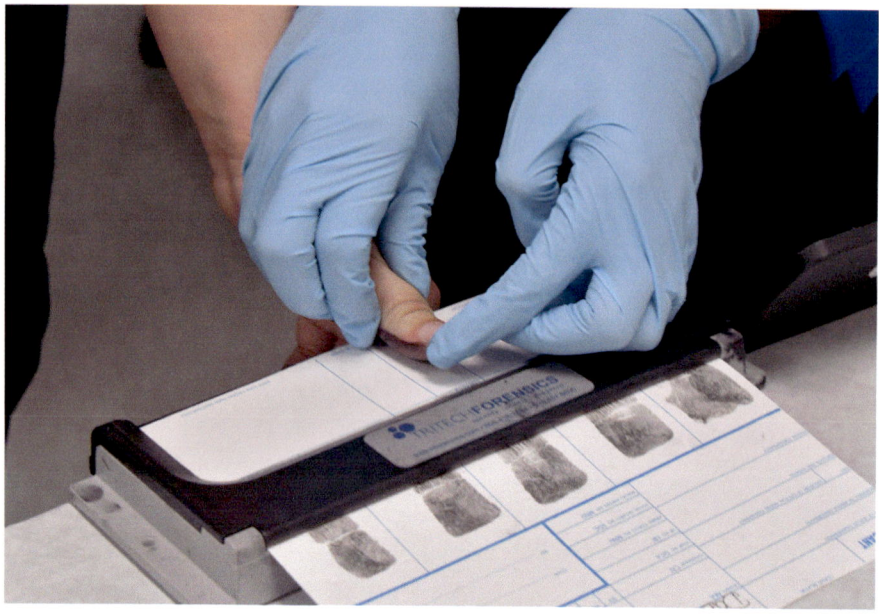

Figure 5.5 Manual fingerprints (flat impressions).

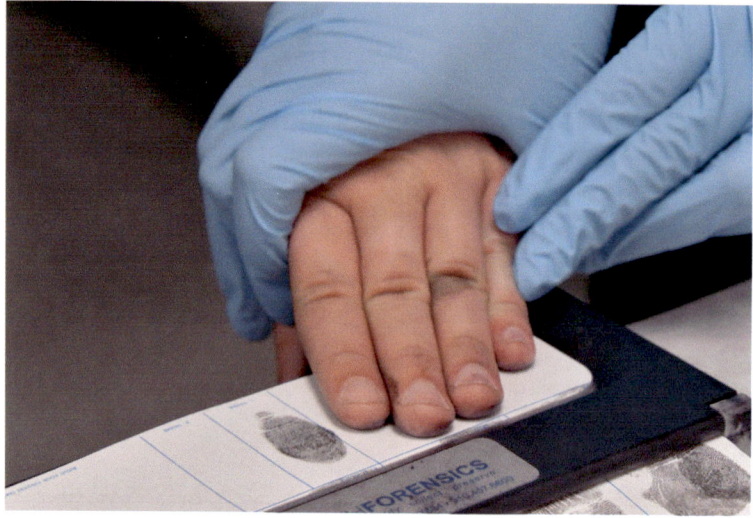

Figure 5.6 Manual (flat impression).

Known/Direct/Inked Fingerprints

        1. Upper ten fingerprint impressions are taken separately and rolled.
        2. Lower impressions are taken simultaneously and are known as plain or flat impressions. Fingers are not rolled. The four fingers of each hand are taken; then thumbs are separately printed.

II. Preparation

    A. Inking the plate

        1. Place a small daub of ink on the plate and use a roller to smoothen ink onto the surface, ensuring the entire plate is covered with a thin film of ink.
        2. Test the amount visually and with your finger. The film should appear almost transparent.

III. Taking the fingerprints (Figures 5.2 through 5.6)

    A. The subject should stand in front of and at the forearm's length from the inking plate.
    B. The person taking the prints should stand slightly to the left of the subject when printing the right hand, and slightly to the right when printing the left hand.
    C. The side of the bulb of the finger is placed on the inking plate and the finger is rolled to the other side until it is entirely covered with ink. The entire bulb should be covered with ink from the tip to below the first joint.

Recording fingerprints with coroner's spoon.

    D. The subject should be cautioned to relax and refrain from trying to help the operator. Oddly enough, the more the subject tries to help, usually the worse the prints will be.

        1. Advise the subject to relax and "look at some distant object."

    E. Rolled impressions (Figures 5.2 through 5.6)

        1. Press the finger lightly on the card and roll from side to side, transferring the ink to the card (*roll from cuticle to cuticle*).
        2. The hand should be rolled from the awkward to the easy position.

            a. The fingers should be *rolled away* from the center of the body.

b. The thumbs should be *rolled toward* the center of the body.
F. Plain impressions (simultaneously lay down four fingers on each hand; Figure 5.6)
1. All fingers should be inked at the same time and pressed onto the card simultaneously. If all four fingers will not fit in the box, then print three fingers and place the fourth on the rear of the card, making note of this on the face of the card.
    a. Before inking the subject, advise the subject to extend their four fingers and hold in that position. Be careful, as some subjects may have a bow to their fingers. If that is the case, advise subjects they are extending too tightly.
2. The thumbs are then inked individually and taken separately. Remember to press down; *do not roll the thumbs*.
G. Taking of palm prints
1. The palm needs to be inked completely. This means the inking roller should be rolled over the entire palm (from fingertips to bottom of palm). The palm is then pressed onto the card. The palm is not rolled. The operator taking the palm print should ensure there is sufficient pressure to record the entire palm, but not too much pressure on the palm, which would cause a smearing effect.
2. The side of the hand (palm) then needs to be inked to record the area known as the writer's palm. Following the procedures mentioned previously, the operator again needs to place the palm onto the card to properly record sufficient information from the side of the palm remembering not to press too hard or move the palm and thereby cause smearing.

IV. Problems in taking fingerprints
   A. Mechanical operation:
      1. Poor impressions are usually caused by
         a. Poor, thin ink
         b. Failure to clean the inking apparatus and finger prior to printing
            i. Alcohol or other commercial preparation may be used.

Known/Direct/Inked Fingerprints

        ii. Perspiring fingers should be wiped dry (perspiring fingers will cause smeared fingerprints).
    c. Failure to completely roll the fingers fully from one side to the other and to ink the whole area from tip to below the first joint
    d. Using too much ink
    e. Insufficient inking
    f. Allowing the fingers to slope or twist resulting in smears and blurs (Note: One of the biggest challenges is to take proper control of the subject being printed.)

B. Temporary disabilities
  1. Fresh cuts or wounds
  2. Bandaged finger or fingers
  3. Occupational issues: Bricklayers, carpenters, secretaries, dishwashers
    a. Try using a small amount of ink
    b. Might also try using softening agents (oils/creams)
  4. Excessive perspiration
    a. Wash hands or wipe with alcohol.
  5. Young children with small ridges. As children get older, the ridges become more pronounced and recording becomes much easier. Generally, children younger than three years old will not leave good prints.

C. Permanent disabilities
  1. Lack of fingers
    a. Note on the card: "Missing at birth."
    b. Note on the card: "Amputated on _____."
    c. If part of the first joint is present, print it.
    d. If all fingers are missing, print the feet.
  2. Crippled or deformed fingers and hands.
    a. If fingers are so deformed that they are touching the palm permanently, note on the card.
    b. In other cases, use spatula, small holder, or curved holder (coroner's spoon).
    c. For fingers of elderly individuals with faint ridges, use a very small amount of ink.

D. Deformed fingers

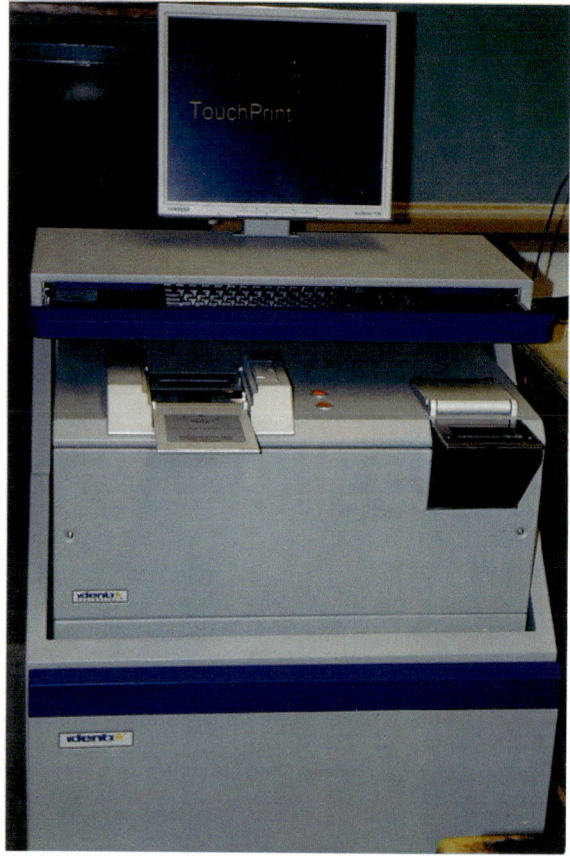

Figure 5.7 Automated fingerprint equipment (live scan).

1. If the subject has more than ten fingers, print the thumb and the next four fingers on the front of the card. Print the remaining fingers on the back of the card. Make note of this on the face of the card.
2. If the subject has webbed fingers, roll as completely as possible and make notation on the card.
3. Split thumbs are classified as if the joint toward the outside of the hand were not present.

Note: Where fingerprints on the rolled impressions are not of sufficient clarity to read or to be scanned into a database, those fingers may use a "Tab Over." The tab over is an adhesive-backed, square tab that may be used to do a reprint of the finger in question. The tab over is placed in the square of the fingerprint to be retaken. There is a caution that must be advised: no more than two tab

Known/Direct/Inked Fingerprints

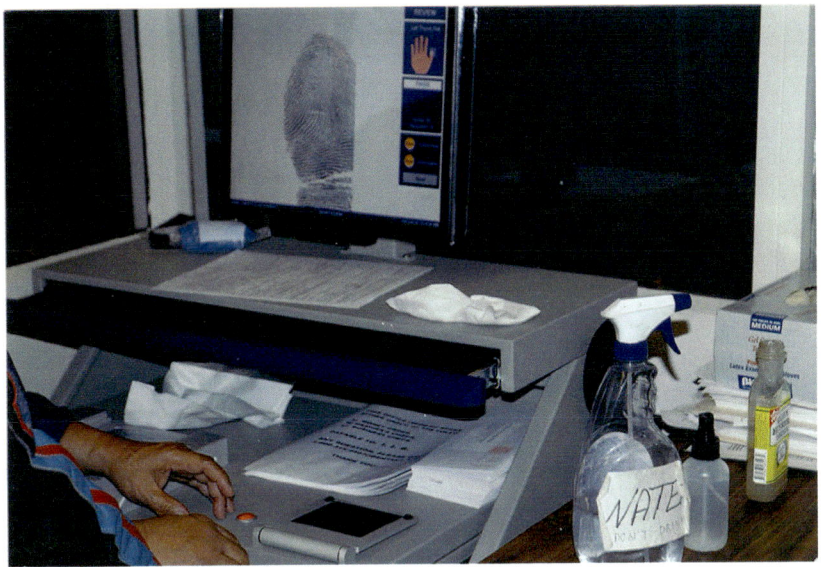

Figure 5.8 Automated fingerprint equipment (live scan).

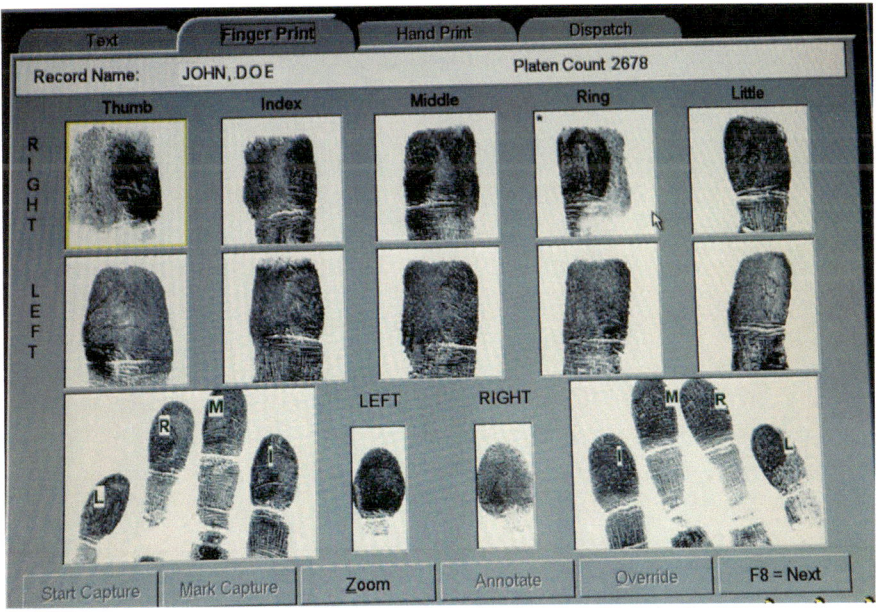

Figure 5.9 Live scan fingerprints.

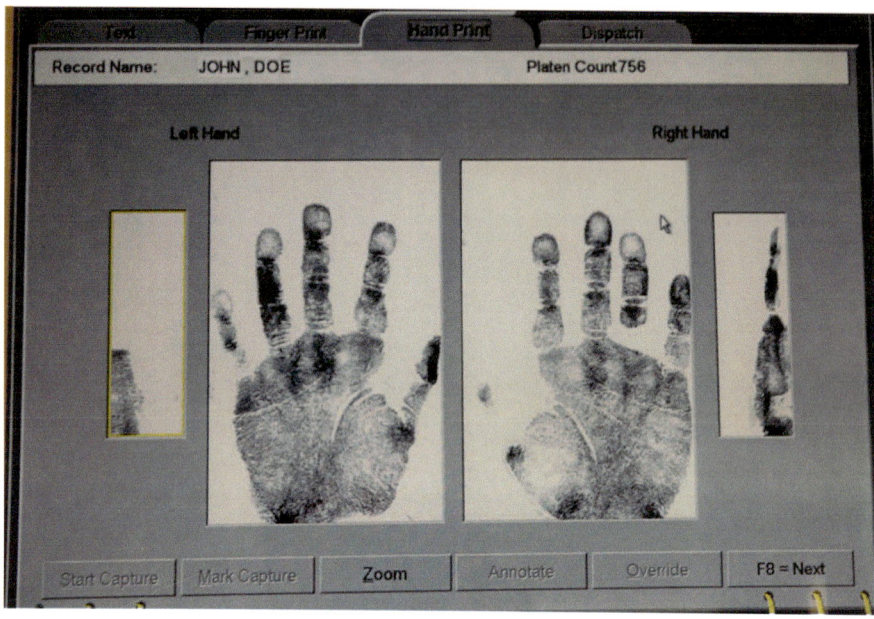

Figure 5.10 Live scan palm prints.

overs may be used on a card or that card will be rejected by the FBI or other agency that will be registering or searching that card in a database.

Live Scan (Figures 5.7 through 5.10)

Live scan prints are basically taken in the same manner as manual fingerprints. However, slightly different protocols must be followed to ensure the quality of the known fingerprint.

With the manual method, proper inking of the prints is accomplished by ensuring the equipment is clean and in order. Live scans must adhere to the same basic principles. With live scans, after a specified number of uses, depending on the system, the system must be checked or recalibrated for accuracy. The printer that is used with the system must also be checked for accuracy to ensure that a quality product is generated. The live scan system automatically records the prints, so the need for extreme accuracy is paramount. Live scan, as the name implies, displays an image on a monitor to the fingerprint operator to register for printing. The main difference between obtaining a live scan print and a manual print is that the live scan print cannot be rolled in the same manner as an inked print. The reader on the live scan system is flat, and therefore the print operator must place the finger on the reader and apply pressure to spread the bulb of the finger onto the reader. Too much pressure and the print becomes smeared. Too little pressure and the entire print will not be captured on the reader. An advantage of the live scan system is that if the operator does not like the print that was registered, that print can be eliminated and retaken before permanent registration onto the fingerprint card. The flat impressions at the bottom of the card are taken in the same fashion as in the manual method. Four fingers are simultaneously taken, then the thumbs. Live scan is considered to be more efficient than the manual method. From personal experience, the author can state that the live scan system is not as messy as the manual method. Both systems share the same challenges and issues when it comes to poor-quality prints and the reasons for obtaining them. As with everything in life, both systems have their advantages and disadvantages. That topic is material for a different discussion.

Unknown Fingerprints (Commonly Referred to as Latent Prints)

Fingerprints are the most common form of physical evidence at crime scenes. Conversely, in some instances, items touched by an individual may not produce latent fingerprints. Fingerprints are extremely fragile and susceptible to damage, so caution needs to be exercised to prevent damage or loss through carelessness. The components of latent fingerprints make them extremely fragile. Latent fingerprints are deposited from a transfer medium in the form of perspiration exuded through the pores and deposited on the friction ridges. Perspiration consists of 95 to 98 percent water and 2 to 5 percent of other chemicals in the body such as chloride, amino acids, and lipids. Most fingerprints developed at crime scenes are partial fingerprints. That fact does not lessen the strength of the evidence. So, whenever fingerprints are developed at the crime scene, it is necessary to obtain elimination fingerprints from all of those who had a legitimate purpose at that scene. What type of fingerprints may be found at a crime scene?

1. *Latent Print:* A chance impression caused by perspiration through the sweat pores on the friction ridges of the skin being transferred to another surface. (In the strictest sense, latent means hidden, and the prints must be chemically enhanced to make them usable and identifiable.) A short note regarding the placement of latent prints is in order at this time. One must consider various factors involved that will dictate if a sufficient latent print will be deposited on a surface. Three things must be present for a quality latent print to be deposited, *a sufficient transfer medium,* a *suitable substrate or surface,* and *appropriate handling of the object.* Oftentimes, a true

latent print may be enhanced through the use of reflective or oblique lighting. This process will sometimes cause the latent to glow somewhat to the point of being visible. The necessary development technique, such brush and powder, may then be applied to render the print usable.
2. *Visible/Patent Print:* An impression caused by ridge detail being transferred in blood, grease, or other foreign substance adhering to the surface or substrate.
3. *Plastic Impression:* An impression resulting from the pressure of the print into a soft surface such as wax, paint, putty, and the like. Ridges will be reversed. The valleys will actually be the ridges, and vice versa. These prints should be photographed or cast and the entire item(s) should be taken as evidence.

Note: Plastic and patent prints are visible to the naked eye and need no enhancement.

What information can be revealed from the presence of fingerprints at the crime scene? What are the limitations of latent fingerprints?

The age of the placement of a latent fingerprint may only be estimated by relationship to other events such as washing, known handling, weather, and the like. The darkness or ready development of a latent print will not be indicative of the age of the print. The latent print itself will not yield the age, sex, or race of the person who deposited the print. An educated estimate may be made by investigators based on their knowledge, training, and experience. An occupational endeavor may affect the appearance of a latent print. Various other conditions can affect not only the deposit but also the appearance of latent prints. General guidelines are listed below. But remember, for every rule, there are always exceptions.

Conditions Affecting Latent Prints

1. *Type of surface:* The best surface is smooth, clean, and glossy or nonporous. Coarse cloth, grained leather, unfinished wood, and stippled surfaces are *generally* poor candidates.
2. *Manner in which the object was touched:* If the finger moves slightly while in contact with the object, ridge detail may be lost or distorted beyond usability. Many times, the pattern area may be smudged but other areas may be clear.
3. *Weather:* May dry out or wash away the print, especially if the print is on an exterior surface.
4. *Humidity:* May cause print to be absorbed into a surface or to dissipate.

5. *Perspiration:* May obliterate print if both ridges and valleys are covered. The more oil deposited with perspiration, the longer the latent will last. Oil is transferred to the fingers from the hairy area of the body. Frequently there is no oil in the perspiration of the finger.
6. *Use of the object:* Was the object simply handled and set down? Was the object used as a weapon? Was the object used as a pry tool?
7. *Care of the suspect:* Most suspects are not concerned about the way in which they handle items. Suspects are usually in a hurry in a burglary or other crime, and as such, they are not careful about what they do and how they do it.

The Crime Scene Search and Fingerprint Development

When arriving at a reported crime scene, generally speaking, the person acting in the capacity of the evidence technician, crime scene analyst, fingerprint analyst, or whatnot will be secondary or tertiary. Providing aid, securing the scene, and conducting preliminary interviews will have already been done by the first responders. However, a good investigator will always be prepared to conduct the appropriate measures where the first unit responder could not or did not provide the necessities of a preliminary investigation.

When the initial process has been completed, the investigator may focus the appropriate resources to develop the physical evidence (fingerprints) that may be present.

A good crime scene management technique will require the investigator to perform four or five tasks, depending on the extent of the scene and the evidence.

1. *Observation:* Do a cursory walk through the scene, preferably with someone who is intimate or familiar with the scene. People live different lifestyles and under varied conditions. The investigator is not there to make judgments on living conditions, but rather to act in the capacity of a professional and identify and develop the evidence.
2. *Evaluation:* What is of evidentiary value? What will be the best method to deal with the evidence? What is the evidence saying? How was the evidence used? Good investigators will ask themselves: "What was touched, used, or altered during the commission of the crime by the suspect, victim, or both?" What are the safety issues associated with the scene and evidence?
3. *Documentation:* How will the scene best be documented? What is important and what is extraneous? Which documentation technique should be utilized—photography, notes, or diagrams? Should all three be utilized? What is being depicted? Will the photographs be a

true and accurate representation of the scene? Do I need to shoot overalls, medium, close up, or identification photos?
4. *Collection:* What should be collected? How will the item be collected? Do I have appropriate containers? Do I have sufficient numbers of containers? What safety issues are involved? Are there bloody prints? Transportation issues?
5. *Analysis:* Which technique will be used? Will the development be better performed at the scene or in a controlled environment? What are the safety considerations?

Throughout one's presence at the scene, one must continually remain vigilant in performing one's duties. For example, whichever method of searching is chosen, that method must be carried out in a methodical, orderly manner. Do not feel rushed. When investigators become anxious, mistakes are made; in some instances, those can never be rectified. Make a thorough search or inspection of those surfaces that have a potential for retaining prints. Pay particular attention to the less obvious. Heavily handled objects, such as doorknobs, may not yield good prints but should not be summarily discarded. Try to view the scene as the suspect did. Take time, weather, and the physical layout of the area into consideration when making your assessment. Psychologically, try to reconstruct the crime for practical direction of a fingerprint search. Generally speaking, the most important area at a crime scene is the point of entry (POE). This is the area where the suspect had to use the most force and energy to gain entry, and the likelihood of the presence of latent fingerprints is greater.

Throughout one's investigation and subsequent development and collection, one must be vigilant regarding two issues that will always be present, the *legal* and *scientific* issues.

Legal issues encompass the Fourth and Fifth Amendments of the U.S. Constitution, specifically issues of search and seizure—the *how* and *what* questions, if you will. In-depth exploration of these issues is reserved for a criminal law or constitutional law class. For our purposes, the main arena of consideration is how was the crime scene or evidence detected, obtained, or developed. Was there a need for a warrant? Whose property is it? Was there an issue of legal standing? Were statements made by a criminal suspect that led to the development of the evidence? Whose premises is it? Was consent required? Was consent properly acquired? Was the chain of custody maintained? Was the integrity of the evidence maintained? These are but a few of the issues that may be considered from the legal perspective of the investigation.

The scientific issues consist of the what and how of the development of the evidence. Various issues arise: What techniques were utilized? What type of training does the investigator possess to perform that technique? Was that training recognized by the forensic community? Are those

Known/Direct/Inked Fingerprints

Figure 5.11 Black powder fingerprint lifting technique.

techniques generally accepted by the forensic community? Does the equipment used meet the forensic standards? Were safeguards in place to prevent contamination of the evidence? What types of containers were used? Are there issues of cross-contamination? Again, the aforementioned are a few of the examples investigators must continually be cognizant of while conducting their investigation and examining the physical evidence.

Fingerprint Development Techniques (see Appendix A)

When choosing a technique to use in the development of latent fingerprints, the technician must recognize the surface on which the fingerprints may have been deposited. Surfaces are categorized as porous (air can pass through such as papers, untreated wood, skin) and nonporous (air cannot pass through it such as plastics, glass, mirror, metals). Textured surfaces, such as leather, also need to be considered. Recognizing the surface type is important when choosing the most effective processing technique in which to yield fingerprints. One must utilize sequential processing. This means that the *least* intrusive method is applied first through to the *most* intrusive. As an example, the least intrusive method is visual examination, using inherent lighting followed by illumination with oblique lighting. The most intrusive would be a dye stain or other chemical technique. Those prints seen without treatment (plastic and patent) should be photographed and, where appropriate, removed from the scene. When photographing, take a photograph with and without a scale of the prints and object. The preferred scale is an ABFO, L scale. To assist in the detection of semi-hidden prints, oblique, infrared, or ultraviolet lighting may be utilized. Prints on non-absorbent, hard surfaces will remain entirely on the surface in the form of a delicate liquid or semisolid deposit consisting mainly of water and oil, extending upward from the surface, which makes an ideal adhesive base for fingerprint powders. Whenever there is a potential of losing the latent print during the lifting or retrieval process, that latent should be photographed.

The following development techniques are not all-encompassing but rather an example of the more common techniques used in the development process. To learn and understand all of the possible methods for development, one must invest many hours in training and practice to perfect the techniques.

Powder Techniques

I. *Brush and Fingerprint Powder Development* (Figure 5.11). This is the most common method of developing latent prints currently in use.

   A. Materials: Fingerprint powder, fiberglass brush, different types of animal hairbrushes, lifting tape, latent cards (black or white and in various sizes), and writing implement.

      1. Apply a small amount to the brush, twirl excess powder off the brush in the powder container. The important thing to remember is that too much powder applied to the latent fingerprint can make identification difficult as the ridges may be filled in due to excessive powder. Gray prints are better than dark black ones.
      2. When applying the brush to the area to be processed, twirl your brush over the area gently touching the surface with the tips of the bristles from the brush. Twirling allows an even distribution of the powder. Gentle application is important here to ensure that we are not brushing away the latent fingerprint. For large areas such as vehicles, applying a layer

Known/Direct/Inked Fingerprints 95

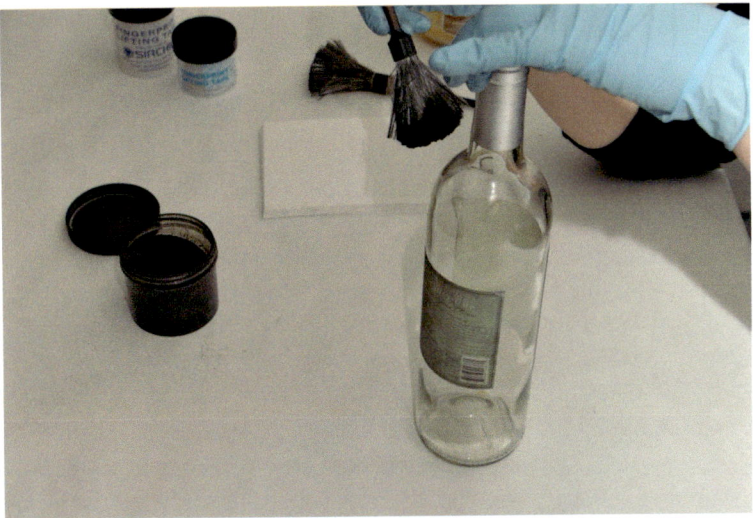

Figure 5.12 Processing with black powder on a nonporous object.

of powder to clean sterile cotton and lightly applying (wiping) the powder to the area is also an acceptable method. Applying the powders to latent (invisible) fingerprints is allowing for them to now be visible so that lifting can be possible.

Be sure the area is dry prior to utilizing the powder technique. If the area is not dry allow the item to dry prior to processing with powder or collect the item (property receipt issued to the owner of the property) and process at the lab.

Figure 5.13 Processing with black powder.

Figure 5.14 Processing with black powder.

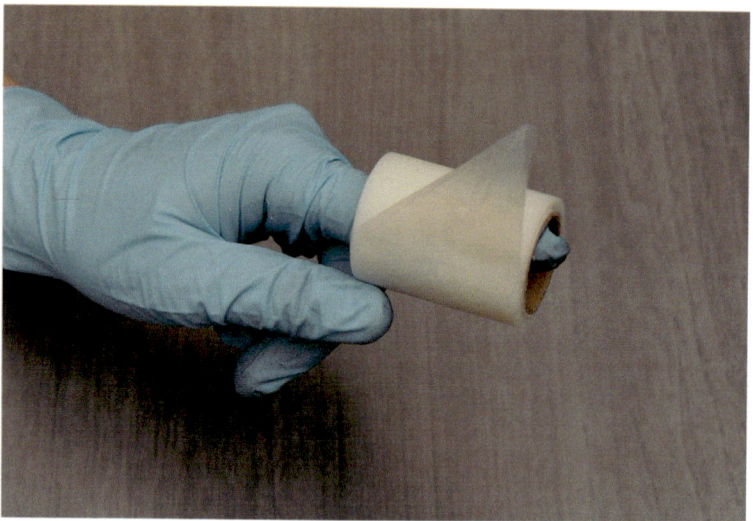

Figure 5.15 Tearing latent tape to leave the triangle on the roll. This prevents technicians from putting their own fingerprints on the sticky side of the tape. Step 1 for tearing latent tape.

Small Particle Reagent (SPR) is another technique (described later) that can be used on wet surfaces.
3. The visible print is then lifted using sterile latent fingerprint tape. To prevent the technician from inadvertently

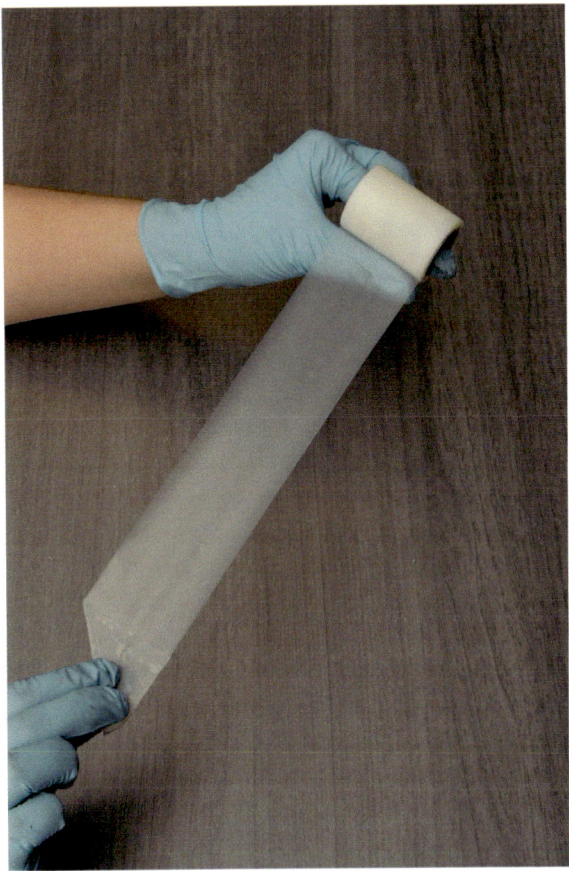

Figure 5.16 Second step in tearing tape to leave a triangle on the tape.

depositing their own fingerprints on the sticky side of the tape, technicians know how to incorporate a triangle at the end of the tape (next to the roll) when tearing the tape off the roll. Once torn from the roll, a triangle remains on the piece of tape which allows the technician to hold the tape without touching the sticky side of the tape (see photographs on how to tear the tape with a triangle later).

With advances in DNA technology, touch DNA can be yielded from fingerprints. The crime scene technician should always carry disposable powders and brushes (one-time use). This prevents contamination from other scenes and allows for any lifted fingerprints to be further evaluated for DNA.

4. Lay the latent tape over the processed (now visible) fingerprint (Figure 5.19), lay this on the unprinted glossy

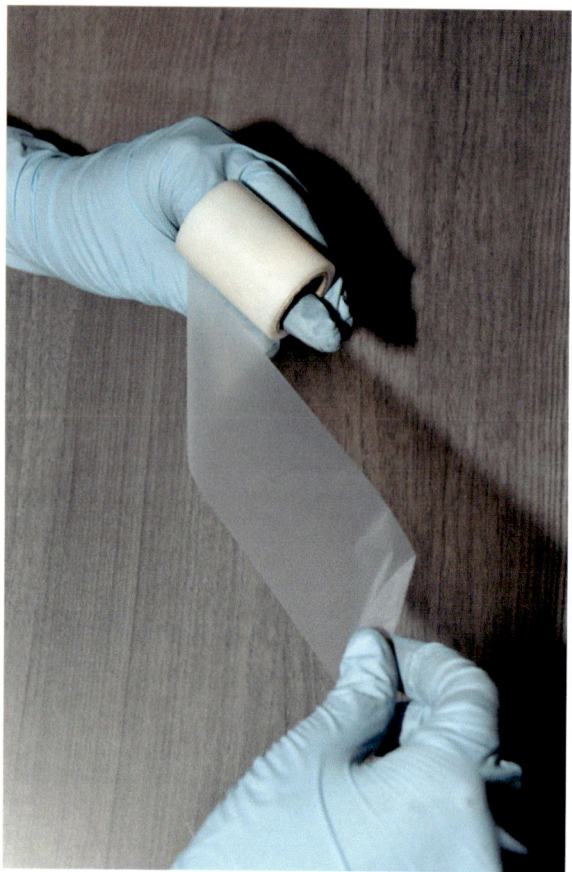

Figure 5.17 Third step in making a triangle on the roll of tape.

side of the card (Figure 5.21). Place the processing technician's initials on an area where no fingerprint characteristics are, between the tape and card ensuring that the tape containing the lifted fingerprint has not been alerted or tampered with (Figure 5.22). Label the other side with case information (case number, type of case, date, location, technician, victim name, and any other pertinent information as per your agency protocols).

II. *Magnetic Powder Development.* This technique is generally not good for prints on metal surfaces or magnetic tapes as the magnet may erase information. This technique works well on porous surfaces.
   A. Materials: Magnetic wand, magnetic particles mixed with powder, lifting tape, latent lift cards, and writing implement.

Figure 5.18 Fourth step in tearing the tape from the roll leaving new triangle on the roll of tape.

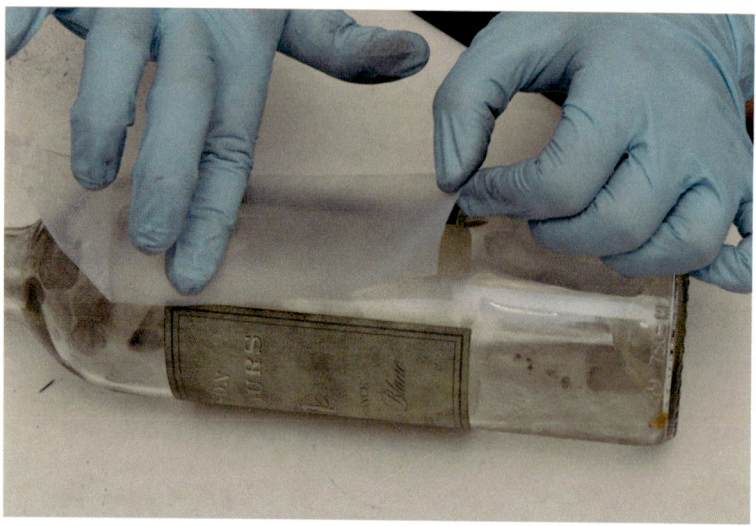

Figure 5.19 Tape with triangle laid over processed fingerprints.

Figure 5.20 Processed fingerprints with black powder on tape.

B. Method: This method is used in a similar fashion as brush and powder. However, the magnetic wand should not touch the surface. The magnetic powder is the only part that should be applied to the surface. The magnetic wand may cause scratches on a surface and degrade or contaminate latent prints. When utilizing the wand, we paint the powder (like a paint brush) onto the surface. The powder only touches, not the wand.

Known/Direct/Inked Fingerprints 101

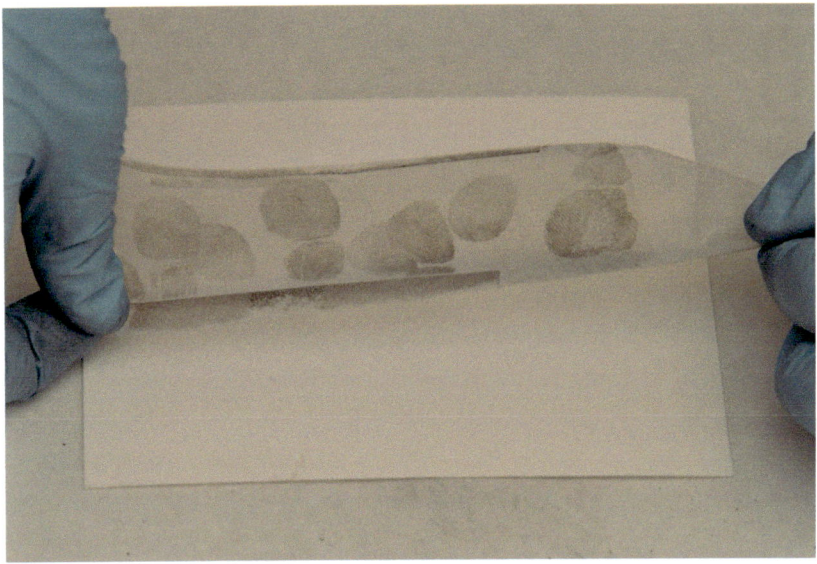

Figure 5.21 Processed fingerprints on tape placed on latent card.

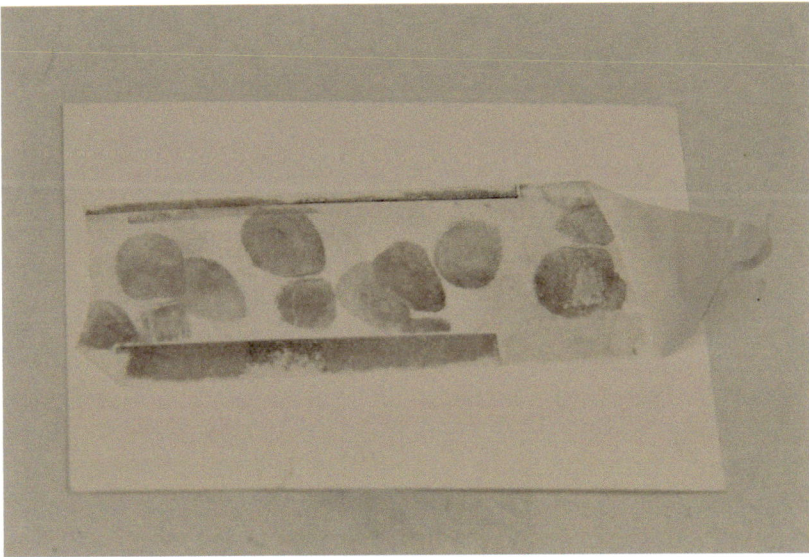

Figure 5.22 Processed fingerprints on the latent card.

Note: There are a variety of powders that may be utilized to develop prints on various surfaces. The most common powders are black, white, and bichromatic. Some powders may also be used in conjunction with other

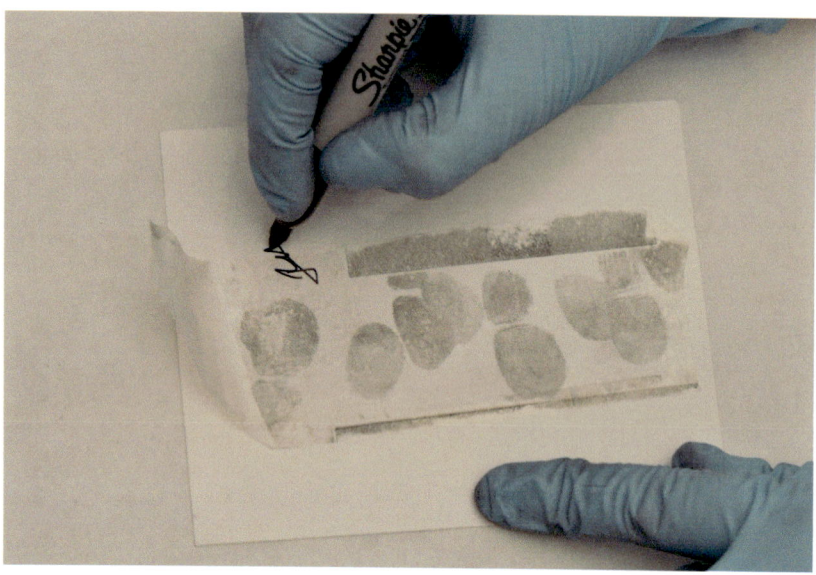

Figure 5.23 Technician's initials across tape and card to ensure the integrity of fingerprint lifts.

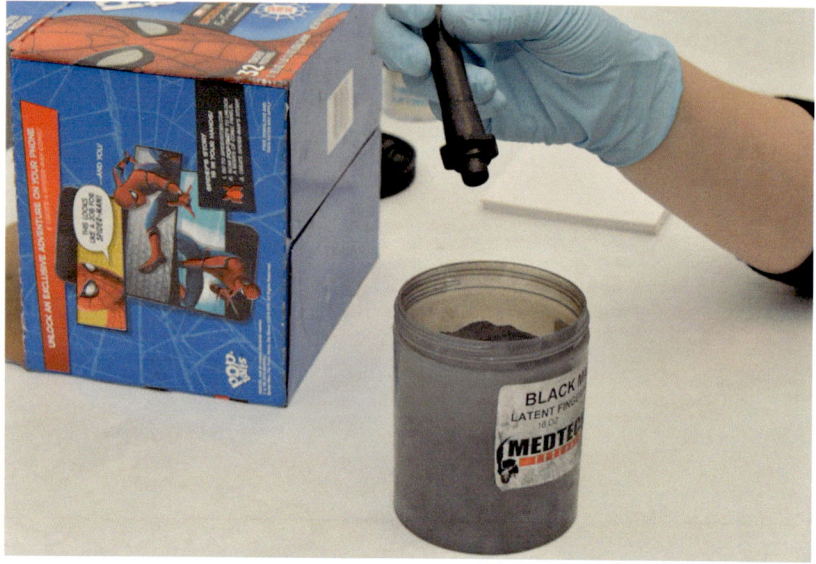

Figure 5.24 Magnetic powder used on porous surfaces (paper, cardboard).

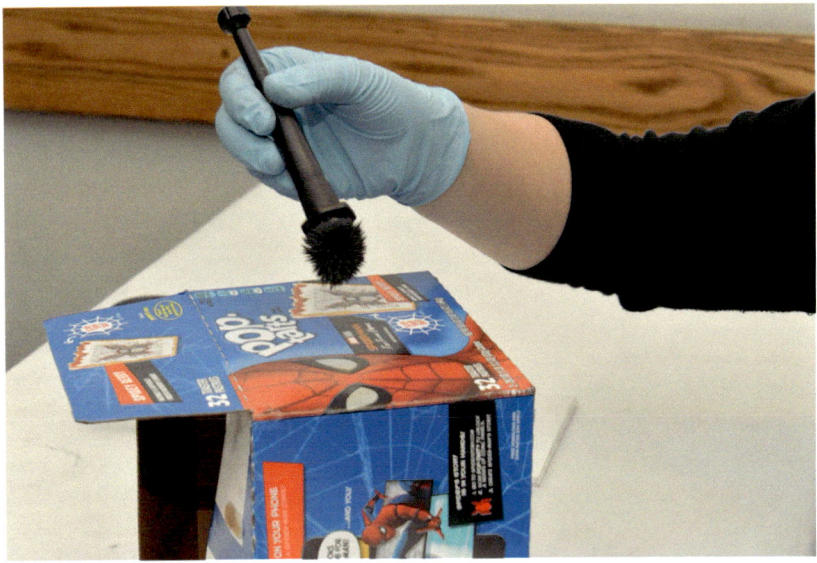

Figure 5.25 Processing with magnetic powder.

Figure 5.26 Processing with magnetic powder on cardboard.

Figure 5.27 Latent tape being laid on developed fingerprint.

chemical techniques such as cyanoacrylate ester (CAE, or Super Glue). The reason for the variety of powders is to provide the greatest contrast with the background on which the fingerprint is developed.

Chemical Techniques

Utilizing various chemicals to develop latent fingerprints allows the investigator the ability to potentially develop prints on any surface if the conditions are right. Which technique to utilize will be dictated by the knowledge and experience of the investigator, as well as the item or surface to be processed. What must be emphasized is that utilizing a specific technique may produce different results in different environments.

When attempting to develop latent prints, there are no absolutes. Remember, latent prints are chance impressions on a surface.

Known/Direct/Inked Fingerprints 105

Figure 5.28 Latent tape and processed fingerprint.

Chemical reactions are a result of substances contained in the perspiration or on the friction skin being transferred from the friction skin ridges to the object. Chemicals such as salt (chloride), protein, amino acids, lipids, and oil react with the chemicals to reveal the latent prints. Other substances might include blood, grease, or food stuffs.

Whatever chemical technique that the technician chooses to use it is important that this technique does not deter from other processing or analysis to be completed (such as DNA). Be sure you understand the usage, hazards in utilizing such chemicals. Asking the manufacturer or the latent examiner will help prior to utilizing chemicals.

Fluorescent Powders

Fluorescent powder is implemented when the surface that contains the possible latent fingerprints are dark or multicolored such as soda cans.

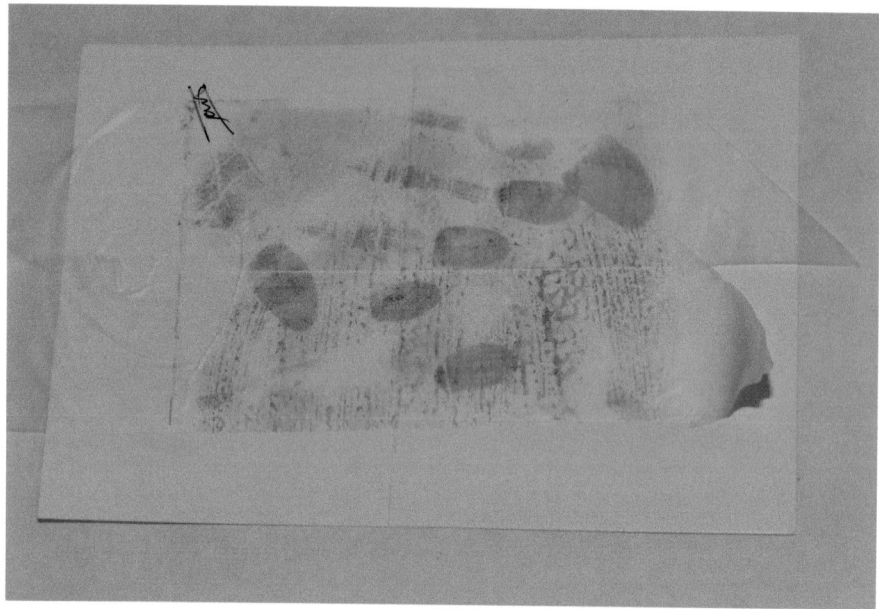

Figure 5.29 Lifted fingerprints on latent fingerprint card.

Black latent cards are effective for placing the tape with the lifted fluorescent fingerprints.

These powders may be used in place of traditional powders or in conjunction with other techniques such as Super Glue (cyanoacrylate). These powders tend to be much finer and produce the best results when used with a feather duster rather than the traditional fiberglass or camel hair brush. The advantage of this technique is that, due to the fine powder composition, less activity is required to develop latent prints, thus lessening the likelihood of destruction of the print. The disadvantage is that with this technique additional luminescence is required in the form of an alternate light source (ALS) or light amplification by stimulated emission of radiation (laser) to make the print usable. Lights with a filter barrier may be used to detect the prints in lieu of the ALS or laser. The prints developed with this method must also be photographed. These powders may be used just as traditional powders are.

Cyanoacrylate Ester

This technique may be used in two methods, the fuming chamber (Figure 5.14) or tenting method, or with a wand. CAE reacts with the amino acids and fatty acids in the perspiration to form a white-colored polymer. Contrast may be enhanced through the use of a variety of powders or dye

Known/Direct/Inked Fingerprints

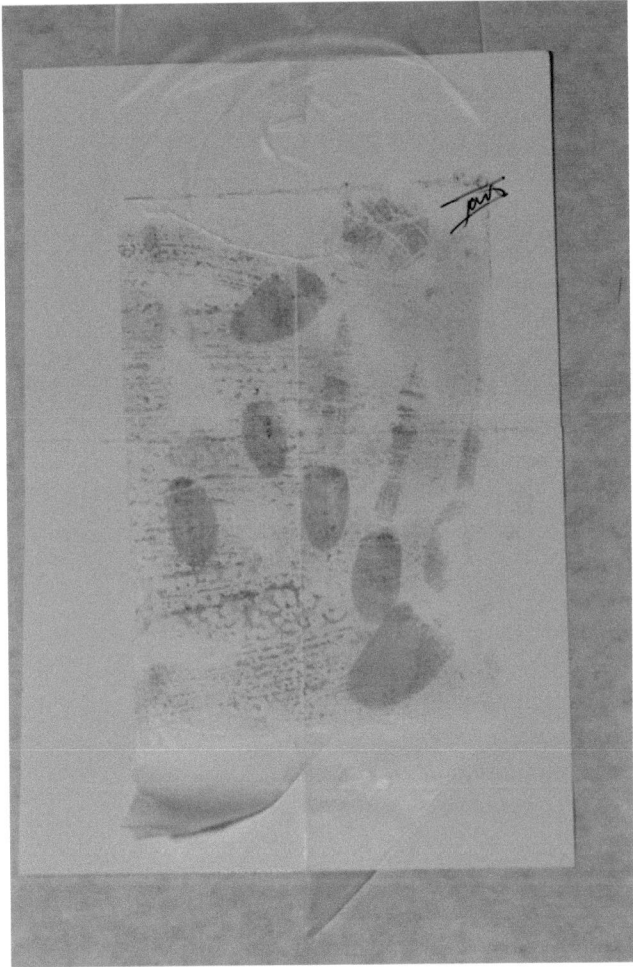

Figure 5.30 Lifted fingerprints on latent fingerprint card with technician's initials.

stains applied to the developed polymer. Commonly, fluorescent powders and dye stains are applied on surfaces where the contrast is less than desirable. An ALS or laser is then used to enhance the print, after which the print is photographed. This method may be applied to metal, glass, plastic, garbage bags, electrical tape, and many other nonporous surfaces.

Caution: When using the CAE method, caution is paramount. This chemical has the same effect as tear gas and may aggravate the mucous glands and membranes.

Figure 5.31 Florescent powders and alternate light source on nonporous objects (fluorescent powders also come in magnetic form to be used on porous objects). Black latent cards assist in viewing results.

Fuming or Tenting Method

Place the specimen, preferably suspended, into a fuming chamber. This allows for the vapors to evenly adhere to the surface(s) of the items. Place ten to twelve drops of liquid CAE into a pipette or aluminum dish that is sitting atop a hotplate or heating device. Heat the CAE, and the vapors should become visible. Where a prepackaged envelope of CAE will be used, simply open the envelope and allow the CAE to disperse into the chamber. Allow the item to remain in the chamber for a minimum of one to two hours. This will allow the CAE to set onto the specimen. To enhance the development process, humidity should be present. Where a chemical reactive process is used, such as sodium hydroxide, place the item to be processed into the chamber. Place cotton treated with sodium hydroxide into an aluminum dish; then add several drops of CAE to the sodium hydroxide-treated cotton. The reaction should be immediate and the vapors will quickly appear. A word of caution, this technique generates a great deal of heat. Some types of hot pad or aluminum should be placed under the cotton to prevent heat damage. To enhance an even dispersal of CAE, a fan should be in the chamber to provide circulation. The fan does not need to be set on high. The purpose is simply to allow the vapors to disperse throughout the chamber. Where there is a large

Known/Direct/Inked Fingerprints

Figure 5.32 Using yellow fluorescent powder on nonporous object.

chamber to be processed, a room or vehicle, the investigator should take the appropriate action to ensure the least amount of contamination occurs.

CAE Wand Method

This method is not as controlled as the chamber method. More care and caution must be exercised. Proper respiratory equipment must be used to prevent contamination. This method is not suggested when processing on a scene. Simply pass the wand over the areas where the suspected fingerprints might be. The prints should quickly develop into a white film on the surface of the item. The fingerprints may then be photographed or further enhanced with the addition of powders. It is suggested that a short period of time (ten to twenty minutes) be allowed to elapse before applying the powder. This will allow the CAE prints to set onto the surface.

Figure 5.33 Yellow fluorescent powder results on nonporous object.

Iodine Fuming

The two most common methods by which this technique may be utilized are the iodine fuming gun (most common) and the fuming cabinet. Two other less used techniques are iodine dusting and iodine solution. When applied, the iodine is absorbed by the fingerprint secretion, which produces a dark brownish to blackish appearance. It is thought that the iodine reacts with fatty acids and lipids contained in the fingerprint. This technique is used for paper and may be used on human skin. This technique is very corrosive and may pose safety issues when improperly applied. The resulting prints that develop must be photographed as the prints tend to fade over time. Fixatives may be applied to iodine-developed prints to prolong their appearance.

Known/Direct/Inked Fingerprints 111

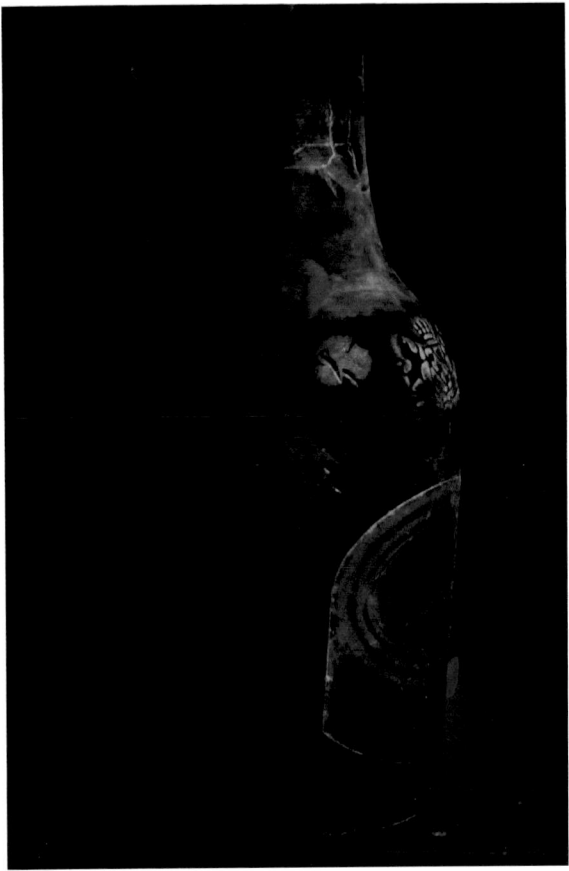

Figure 5.34 Yellow fluorescent powder results on nonporous object utilizing an alternate light source.

Fuming Gun

Constructing a fuming gun requires a glass or hard plastic tube with a small rubber hose used as a nozzle applicator. Iodine crystals, glass wool, and calcium chloride are placed into the gun. To activate the iodine, blow into the mouthpiece and move the nozzle or rubber hose over the object where fingerprints are thought to be. The heat from the breath will activate the chemicals. When the fingerprints develop, they should be noted and photographed as soon as possible to prevent the possibility of loss. Upon completion of the technique, the equipment should be cleaned as soon as possible to prevent corrosion.

Fuming Cabinet

Suspend the items to be treated in a cabinet at the upper portion. Place the iodine crystals in a clean evaporating dish inside the cabinet. Close the door

Figure 5.35 Pink fluorescent powder results on nonporous object utilizing an alternate light source.

to the cabinet. The crystals are then heated within the cabinet. Keep the items in the cabinet under observation to monitor the development of latent prints. When maximum contrast has been achieved, remove the remaining crystals from the cabinet. Then remove the items from the cabinet and, as soon as possible, photograph the prints on the item.

Ninhydrin Method

Ninhydrin is a solution that may be applied by using a spray, swabbing, or dipping method. Ninhydrin may be commercially purchased or can be prepared by the investigator. Ninhydrin reacts with the amino acids, peptides, and protein contained in the print. This chemical is used on items such as paper, cardboard, and unfinished wood. The reaction of the chemical produces what has been termed Ruhemann's Purple. This is a pinkish/purple color print that appears on the item revealing the presence of fingerprints. The processing of an item with this method should be completed in a controlled laboratory setting. Appropriate breathing apparatus and proper ventilation should be utilized as well as thick rubber gloves. This chemical should not be inhaled, nor should the chemical be allowed to contact the skin. The preferred method of application of this chemical is by dipping or swabbing. This alleviates the possibility of accidental inhalation. To enhance or provide optimal development of ninhydrin prints, the item should be placed in a chamber where the temperature and

Known/Direct/Inked Fingerprints

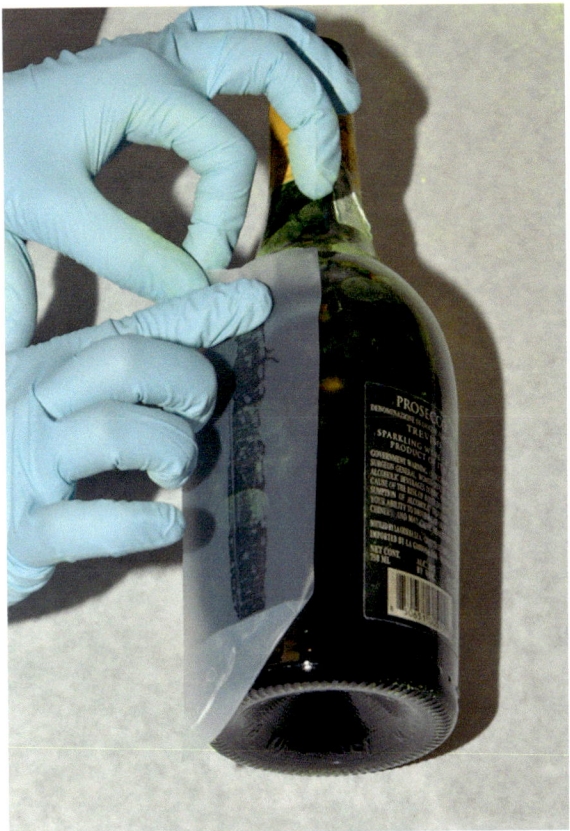

Figure 5.36 Latent tape on results for lifting purposes.

humidity are sufficient. The desired temperature is approximately 80°F, with a humidity rate of approximately 80 percent. For quicker results utilizing a warm iron will help. However, be sure to place clean white paper above and below the item to prevent contamination of the item.

DFO (1,8-Diazafluoren-9-one)/PD (Physical Developer)

Both of these techniques are used on paper or cardboard items. Both techniques are best used through dipping or swabbing the piece of evidence. The evidence should then be placed into a chamber where the fingerprints will be allowed to develop. These techniques are utilized in much the same way as ninhydrin. These chemicals will also necessitate the use of an ALS or laser. The reaction is with amino acids, peptides, and protein contained in the print.

1,2-Indanedione Reagent

1,2-Indanedione Reagent is a chemical alternative for DFO in chemical processing for latent prints on porous surfaces and is generally utilized

Figure 5.37 Results from cyanoacrylate.

prior to processing with ninhydrin. Although DFO is an excellent reagent, there are certain limitations to the DFO method, such as the high cost. 1,2-Indanedione Reagent reacts with the amino acids in fingerprint residues and produces fluorescent products that render latent prints visible (Medtech Forensics).

MBD
MBD is a dyestain consisting of MBD dye, 4-(4-methoxybenzylamino)-7-nitrobenzofuran, in a mixture of organic solvents. MBD has been noted to be an excellent dye for cyanoacrylate-developed prints on nonporous objects.

Nile Red Dye Stain
Nile Red Dye Stain is often used after cyanoacrylate processing on multi-color surfaces. Nile Red is fluorescent when exposed to a forensic light source between 450 nm and 560 nm, making it ideal for use with a wide variety of forensic light sources (Evident).

Known/Direct/Inked Fingerprints

Figure 5.38 Super glue fingerprint processing techniques. Example of a fuming chamber that is utilizing the technique known as CAE, common name: Super Glue. The fuming chamber method is a preferred method as it keeps the vapors generated by the CAE technique contained, preventing unintentional contamination.

Oil Red O (ORO)

Oil Red O (ORO) is a lipid stain that is used for enhancing latents produced by the lipids commonly found in foodstuffs, oils, cosmetics, and other fatty substances. Oil Red O has been found to be particularly useful in revealing latents on porous surfaces that have been wet, a process that normally removes the amino acids, salts, etc., which are the basis of conventional chemical processing methods. Compared with physical developer, the ORO technique is much less complex and gives results of impressive clarity and

Figure 5.39 Super glue fingerprint processing techniques.

intensity. Oil Red O is a very useful and successful method of latent development and is used last in the sequence of chemical development techniques (Medtech Forensics).

R.A.M. Dye Stain—Rhodamine, Ardox, and MBD

R.A.M. Dye Stain is a fluorescent stain mixture of Rhodamine 6G, Ardrox, and MBD. Use R.A.M. with a forensic light source after processing with cyanoacrylate. Particularly, it is useful in the enhancement of cyanoacrylate developed prints on plastic bags. R.A.M. enhanced latent prints are visualized between 415 nm and 530 nm, making it ideal for use with a wide variety of forensic light sources. Provided as a 32 oz. premix bottle or concentrate (mix concentrate with 1 L of solvent (Evident)).

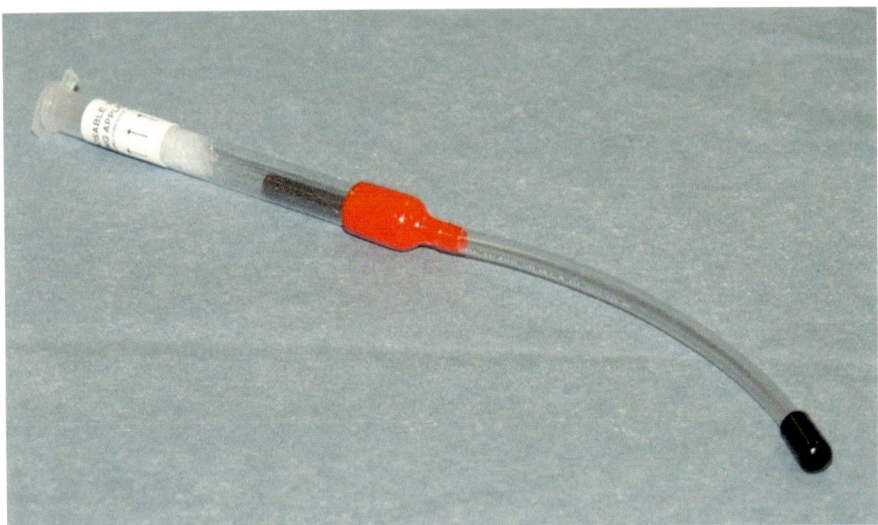

Figure 5.40 Iodine fuming.

Figure 5.41 Ninhydrin on paper.

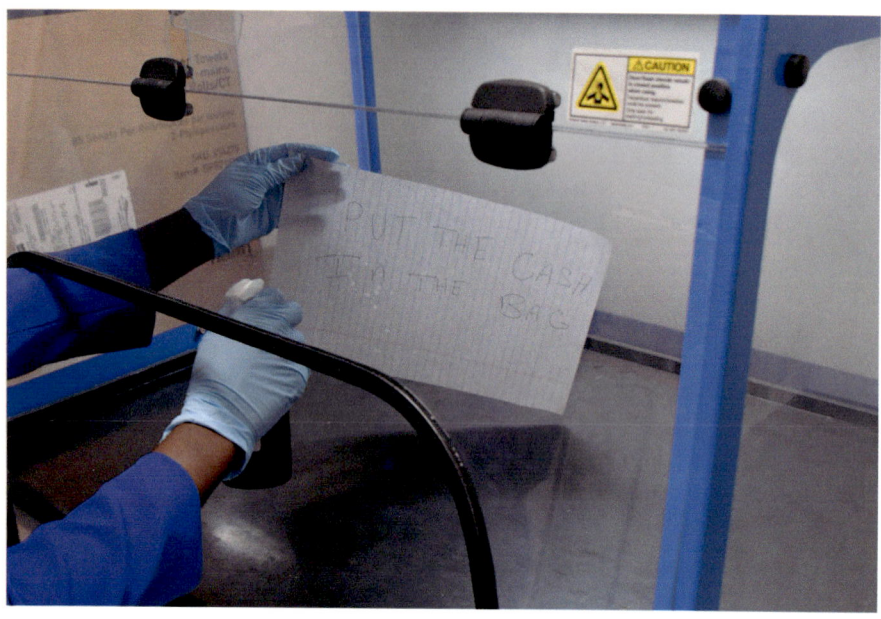

Figure 5.42 Spraying Ninhydrin on paper using a hood.

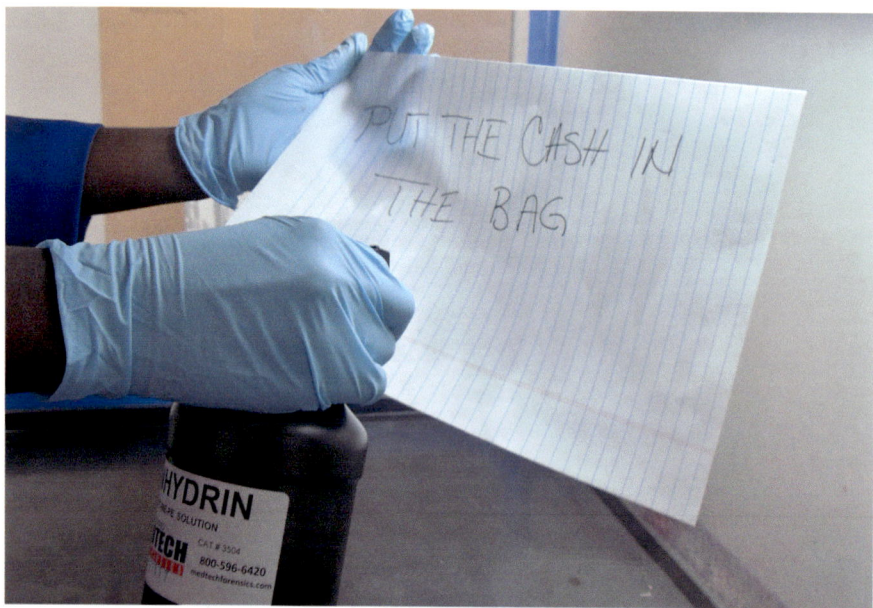

Figure 5.43 Sprayed Ninhydrin on paper.

Known/Direct/Inked Fingerprints

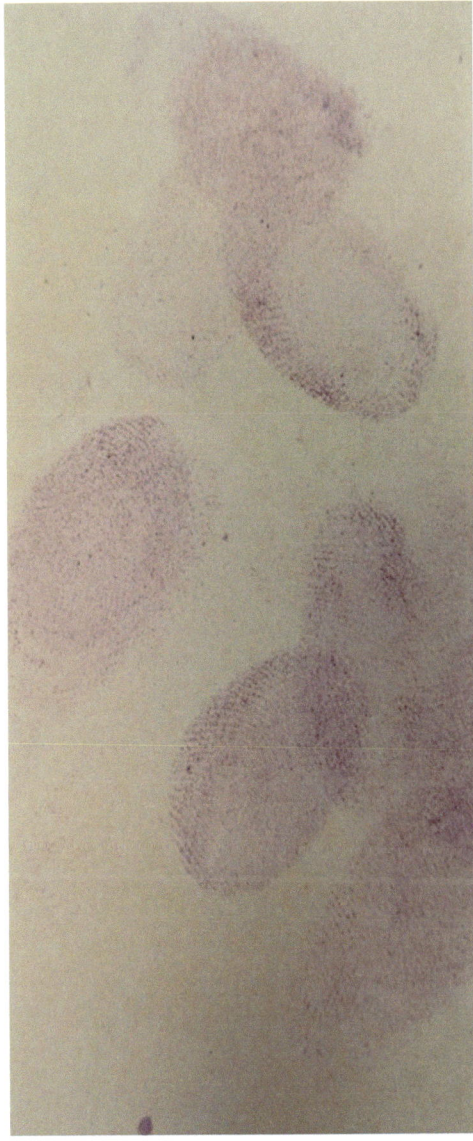

Figure 5.44 Results of sprayed Ninhydrin.

Rhodamine

Rhodamine Premix is a dye consisting of Rhodamine 6G dye in a mixture of organic solvents. Rhodamine has been noted to be an excellent dye for cyanoacrylate developed prints. Longwave UV, Laser, or ALS is a suitable light source in order to visualized dyed prints (Medtech Forensics).

Figure 5.45 DFO (Source: Adorama Camera Inc.).

Ardrox Dye Stain—Alcoholic Premix

This fluorescent spray is designed for enhancing latent prints that have been developed with cyanoacrylate. It provides excellent ridge detail when the latent print is saturated with Ardrox. Prints fluoresce yellow/green when viewed under a light source (Evident).

Ardrox Dye Stain—Aqueous Premix

This fluorescent spray is designed for enhancing latent prints that have been developed with cyanoacrylate. It provides excellent ridge detail when the latent print is saturated with Ardrox. Prints fluoresce yellow/green when viewed under a light source (Evident).

Basic Yellow 40 Dye Stain

Basic Yellow 40 Dye Stain is designed to enhance latent fingerprints developed with cyanoacrylate on non-fluorescent, multi-colored surfaces.

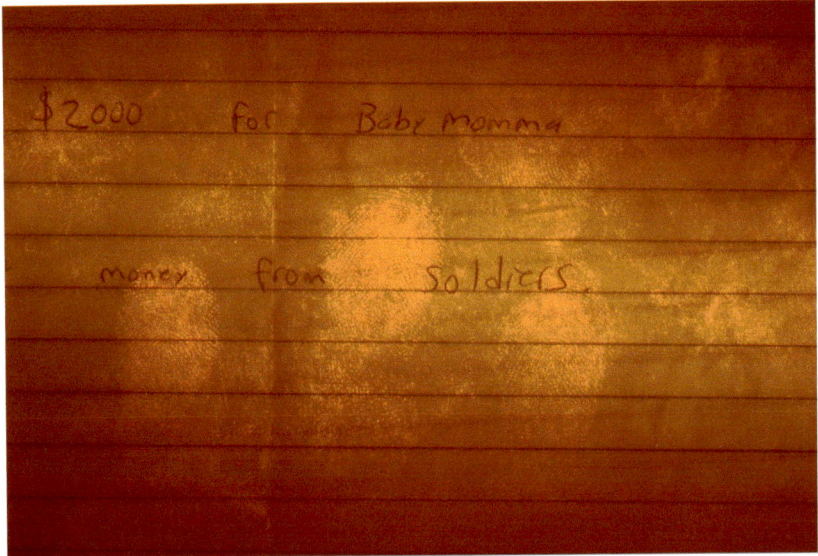

Figure 5.46 Results of DFO (Courtesy of Johan Bravo).

Prints fluoresce bright yellow/green between 365 nm and 485 nm with a forensic light source or a UV light (Evident).

Crystal Violet (Gentian Violet)

Crystal Violet (Gentian Violet) is commonly used for developing latent prints on the adhesive side of virtually all types of tape. A simple solution of Crystal Violet and water will produce impressive results. Crystal Violet may be applied by either dipping or brushing the solution onto the adhesive side of tape (Evident).

Sticky Side Powder®

These techniques are used on sticky surfaces. The most common type of surface that these techniques apply to are adhesive tapes (masking, duct, packaging). Gentian violet is used by dipping the item into a bath of the material. Sticky Side Powder may also be used in a bath, or by painting the adhesive surface. Both techniques involve multistep processing when examining tape. Tape has a shiny side, which should be processed for fingerprints before applying either technique. Appropriate safety gear is a must when using either of these techniques. As an example, should Gentian violet contact the skin, the skin will turn purple almost immediately. This is a reaction to the amino acids in the skin. The reaction will not come off quickly. It must wear off. Again, proper safety procedures must be undertaken when utilizing fingerprint development techniques.

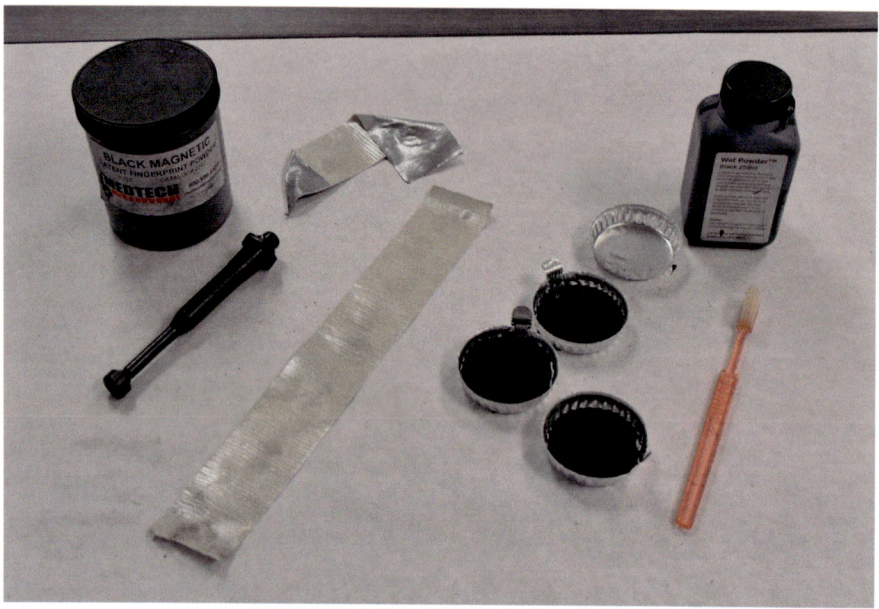

Figure 5.47 Sticky side technique for the sticky side of tapes. Magnetic powder to be used on the nonstick side of tapes.

Small Particle Reagent (SPR) is a commonly utilized method to develop latents on wet or difficult surfaces such as rusty metal, rocks, painted concrete, textured glass, heavily oxidized vehicle paints, and sticky soda cans. It particularly excels in processing vehicles that are wet due to rain or dew.

Analogs That React with Blood

Where it is suspected there may be latent fingerprints in blood, and those prints may not be clearly visible, chemical techniques may be applied to enhance the appearance of fingerprints. Proper safety and care must be exercised when using the following techniques. The analogs are best used in aerosol form. This means that masks and gloves should be worn to protect the user against unnecessary contamination.

Coomassie Blue

When sprayed on the suspected area, the prints will turn dark bluish-black.

Leucocrystal Violet

Per Medtech Forensics, Leucocrystal Violet is commonly used to enhance bloodstained fingerprints and footwear impressions. Leucocrystal Violet will not enhance a print composed solely of normal latent print residues,

Known/Direct/Inked Fingerprints

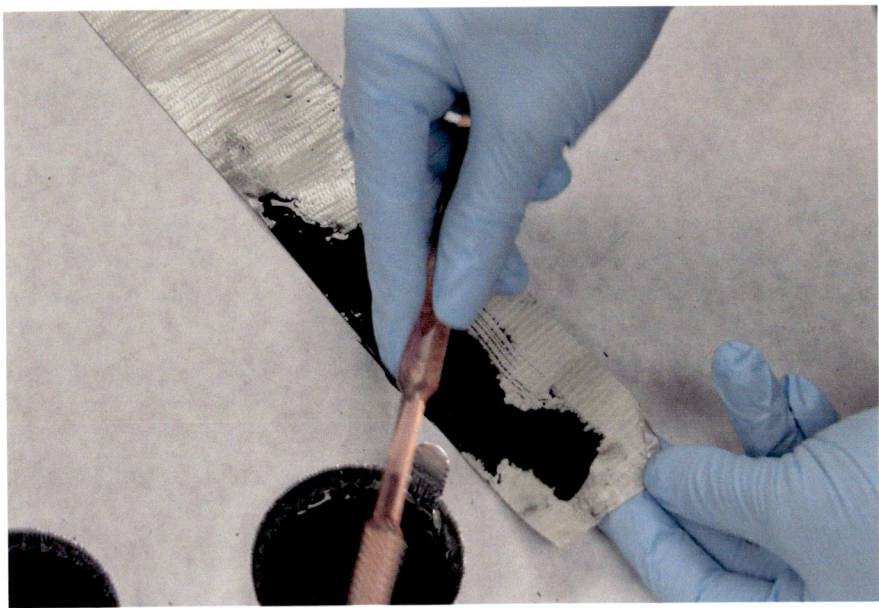

Figure 5.48 Sticky side technique.

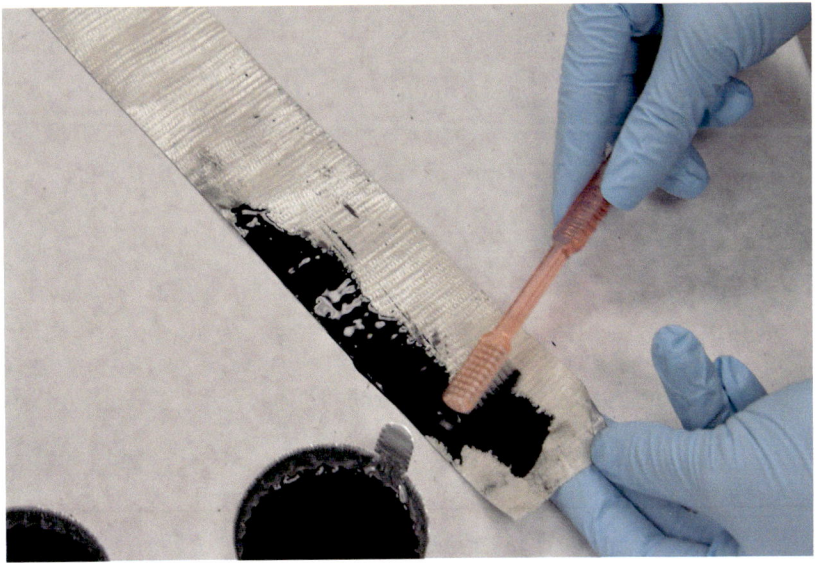

Figure 5.49 Sticky side technique.

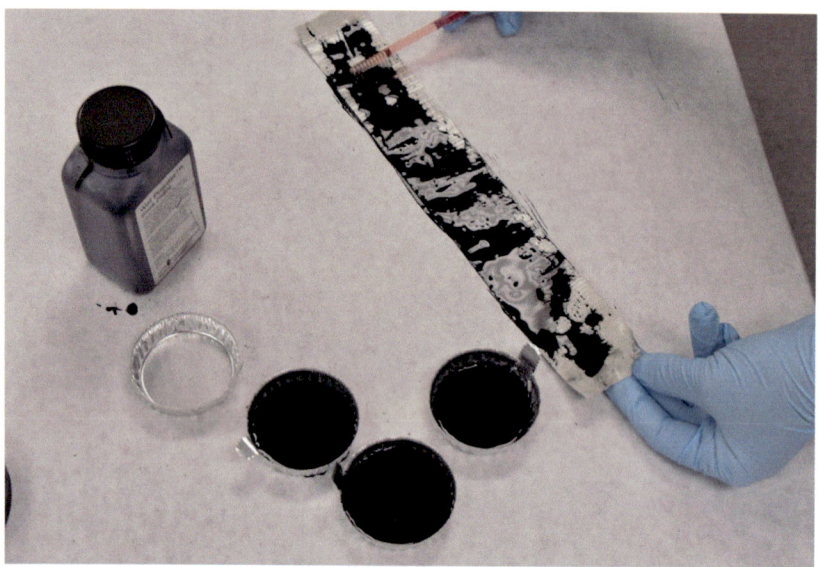

Figure 5.50 Sticky side technique.

so it is used only in cases with blood-contaminated impressions. LCV is nearly colorless when first mixed, but is oxidized by the catalytic action of hemoglobin in the bloodstain, and will convert to a blue-colored solution, which will then stain the bloodstain. Premixed Leucocrystal Violet solution is an aqueous mixture containing Hydrogen Peroxide in addition to other chemicals. Always use in a fume hood or with other adequate ventilation and wear protective gloves and eyewear. Leucocrystal Violet can stain clothing and skin, so be careful. Read and follow the MSDS sheet.

Sudan Black
Per Arrowhead Forensic, Sudan Black is a dye that stains the fatty components of sebaceous sweat to produce a blue-black image. While Sudan Black is less sensitive than some other latent print development techniques, it is particularly useful on surfaces contaminated with grease, food residue, or dried soft drink deposits. It is also quite useful as a dye stain for cyanoacrylate developed prints. Sudan Black may be used on nonporous surfaces such as glass, metal, and plastics particularly if these surfaces are contaminated with greasy or oily materials. Sudan Black is not suitable for use on porous surfaces like paper, cardboard, or raw wood. Its principal advantages are its relatively inexpensive cost and its effectiveness on surfaces so badly contaminated that powders are inappropriate.

Known/Direct/Inked Fingerprints

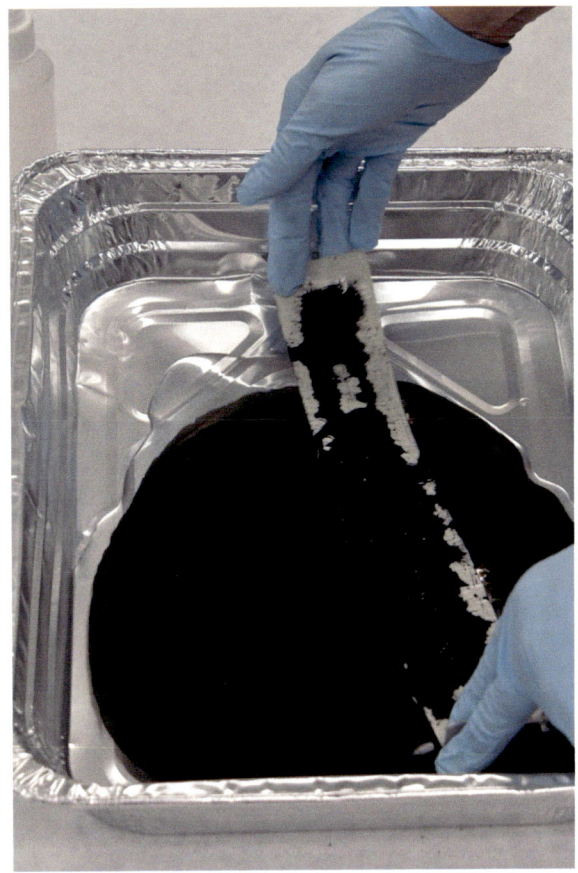

Figure 5.51 Rinsing tape agitating in distilled water.

Blue Star

Per Evident, Bluestar Forensic Blood Reagent is a blood enhancement reagent whose purpose is to reveal bloodstains that have been washed out, wiped off, or are invisible to the naked eye. This product is intended for crime scene investigators. Based upon chemiluminescence, the unique formula qualifies it as the most effective blood reagent available on the market for crime scene, as well as forensic lab use. Bluestar Forensic does not alter the DNA of the revealed blood which allows for subsequent comparison. Bluestar is non-toxic and easy to prepare and apply.

Fluorescein

Per Evident, Fluorescein causes a catalytic reaction to occur between the hemoglobin in blood and oxygen. This reaction produces a luminescent

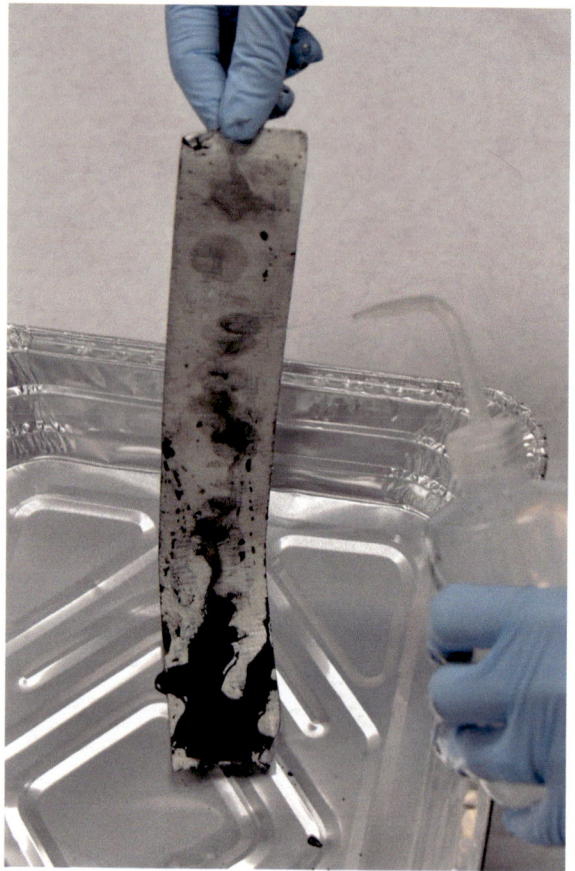

Figure 5.52 Another technique for rinsing chemical from tape.

stain which will luminesce in the dark when excited with UV or ALS. The major advantage of Fluorescein is that it will continue to luminesce for hours under UV or ALS after the initial application, and without additional applications of the reagent. This product is commonly used to detect blood spatter, bloodstained fingerprints, and footwear impressions, as well as, blood evidence which has been concealed or cleaned.

Luminol/Bluestar: When sprayed on the suspected area, the prints will fluoresce. The challenge with this technique is that it must be undertaken in a darkened environment. Luminol prints must be photographed at the time of fluorescence because when luminol stops reacting with the blood, the prints will no longer be visible.

With all of the blood analogs, photographs should be taken immediately to record the prints. Certain items may be taken into custody,

Known/Direct/Inked Fingerprints

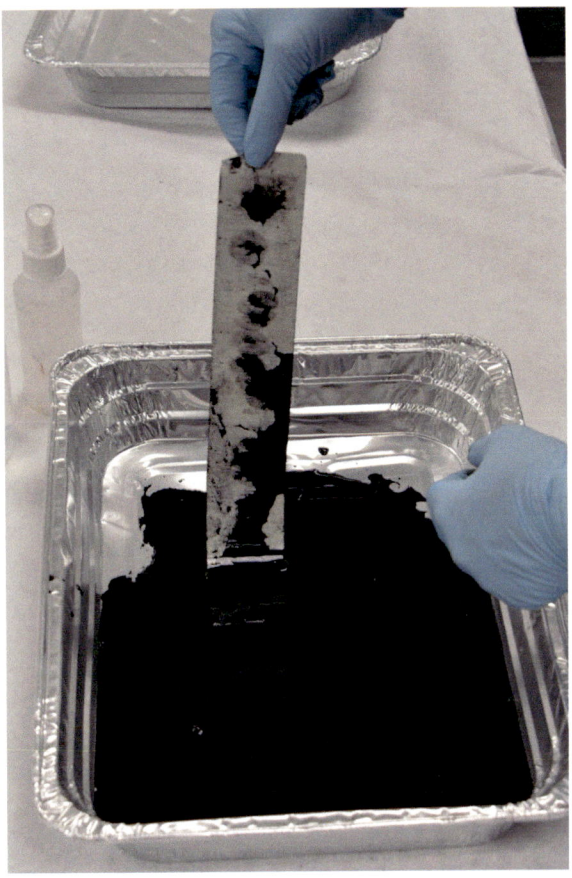

Figure 5.53 Tape in water yielding results.

while other items may have to be left at the scene depending on the circumstances.

As a reminder, when deciding which method(s) to choose, always utilize *sequential processing*.

Sequential Processing (Guide)
1. Available light (ambient light/flashlight/ALS/ultraviolet)
2. Powder(s)
3. DFO
4. Ninhydrin
5. Dye stain

Procedure after Developing Prints
1. Photograph where appropriate. The photos should be done with and without a scale. The best type of scale is the ABFO, L type of scale.

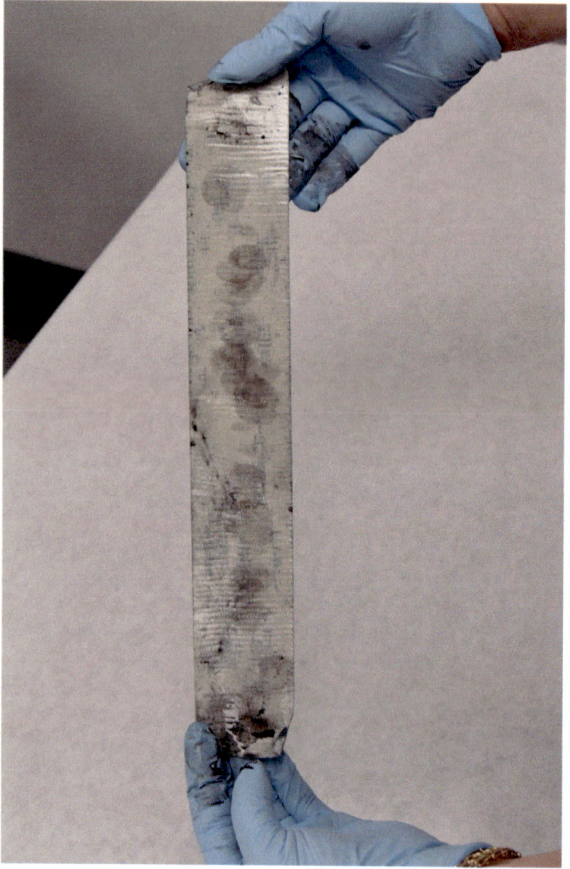

Figure 5.54 Tape yielding results.

Overalls of the item where the print was developed should be taken, as well as close-ups showing the print itself. If possible, a one-to-one photo should be taken.
2. Upon completion of the photography, the decision must be made whether the entire item will be taken or whether the print will be lifted from the item. When appropriate, the entire item or object should be retained for use in court. Note: Remember, the print is the evidence, not necessarily the surface that the print was developed from.
3. Where a lift is made and placed onto a latent fingerprint lift card, the following information should be present:
   a. Case/report number
   b. Date/time

Figure 5.55 Small Particle Reagent and wet objects.

    c. Scene address
    d. Person making the lift
    e. Type of object
    f. Place of lift (Note: A sketch should be made on the card near the lift)
4. Take elimination prints from victims, and witnesses where appropriate.
5. Care and transportation of the evidence:
    a. Ensure the chain of custody is recorded to provide accountability.
    b. If items need to be secured, ensure proper securing of the item's by top and bottom, or in a place least likely to damage the item or fingerprints.

Figure 5.56 Wet object.

Figure 5.57 Spray Small Particle Reagent on wet object.

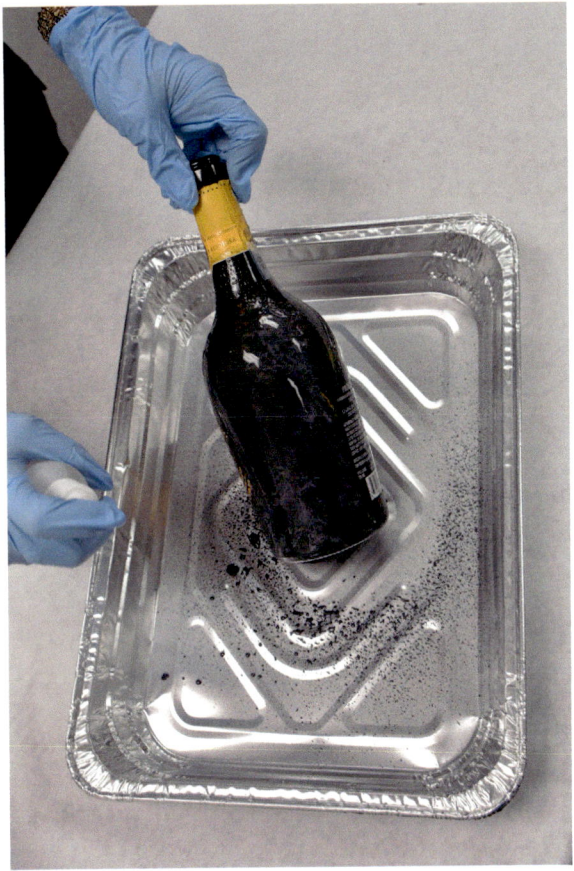

Figure 5.58 Spray Small Particle Reagent on wet object.

Fingerprint Comparison and Identification

Comparison: The observation that two impressions have ridge characteristics of *similar* shapes that occupy the same *relative* positions in both patterns (Figure 5.16).

Identification: The process of determining that the same finger made two or more fingerprint impressions based on the friction ridge details of both impressions (Figure 5.17).

When a fingerprint lift is made, the latent print examiner must conduct a comparison, where appropriate, in hopes of effecting an identification. When latent fingerprints are developed, the best choice for comparison will be determined by the latent print examiner. For example, where groups of three fingers are developed and submitted, the likely choice for comparison

Figure 5.59 Spray Small Particle Reagent on wet object.

is the index, middle, and ring fingers. Where loop patterns are submitted, loops opening to the right are probably from the right hand, and loops opening to the left are probably from the left hand. Double loop whorl patterns are most common to the thumbs. Central pocket loop whorls are most common to the ring finger. The index fingers show the widest variation in patterns of all the fingers. There are also characteristics that may indicate to the latent print examiner that in fact the print submitted may not be of a finger but rather from a palm or even a toe or foot. Various characteristics that present themselves on a latent print, to the trained eye, will be indicative of a certain part of the anatomy. This advanced training is crucial to the latent print examiner.

However, if the latent print examiner does not have a known exemplar to compare with, entering the latent fingerprint into the database or AFIS (Automated Fingerprint Identification System) will be the alternative. A short discussion about AFIS is in order at this time. The term *AFIS* is a misnomer, unfortunately. An AFIS is nothing more than an elaborate filing and searching system. An AFIS does not make identifications. The identification is the purview of the latent print examiner. The latent print examiner enters the appropriate information into AFIS then allows the system to search the database. When the search is complete, AFIS will give a list of potential candidates to search against. That list can be any number designated by the operator of the AFIS. It is then the job of the latent print

Known/Direct/Inked Fingerprints   133

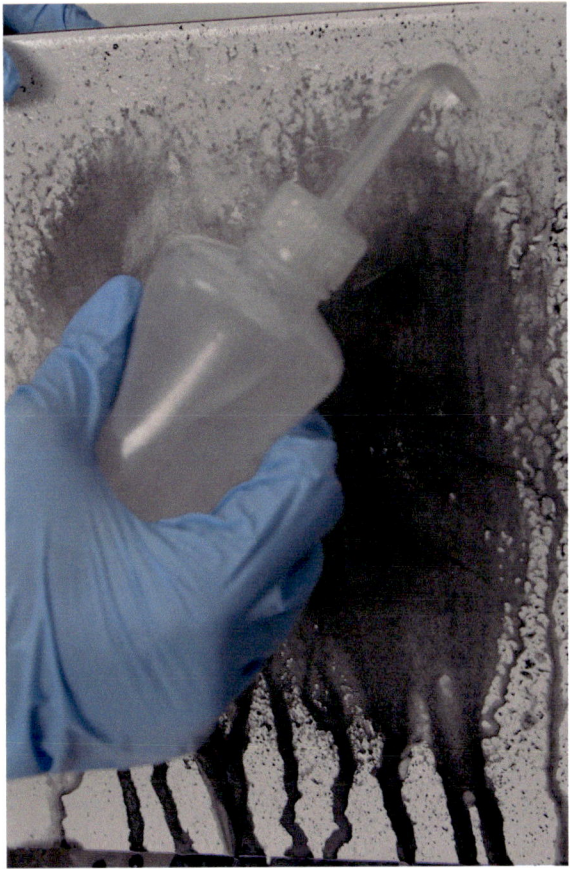

Figure 5.60 Rinse Small Particle Reagent on wet object with distilled water.

examiner to begin with the first candidate on the list and use the comparison process until and if identification is rendered. In some instances, identification will not be made. Like anything else, sometimes the appropriate information has not yet been entered into AFIS. Specifically, if a person has not been booked and their fingerprints taken, those prints will not be in the AFIS (Figure 5.15).

Since the advent of AFIS, countless hours of searching have been eliminated. AFIS can now do in seconds what used to take literally months under the manual system of filing and searching. Additionally, partial latent fingerprints can now be searched as a matter of routine. Today, AFIS has become a standard piece of forensic fingerprint identification equipment.

The *comparison* process that has been established requires diligence and an eye for detail. Trained examiners know the awesome responsibility that

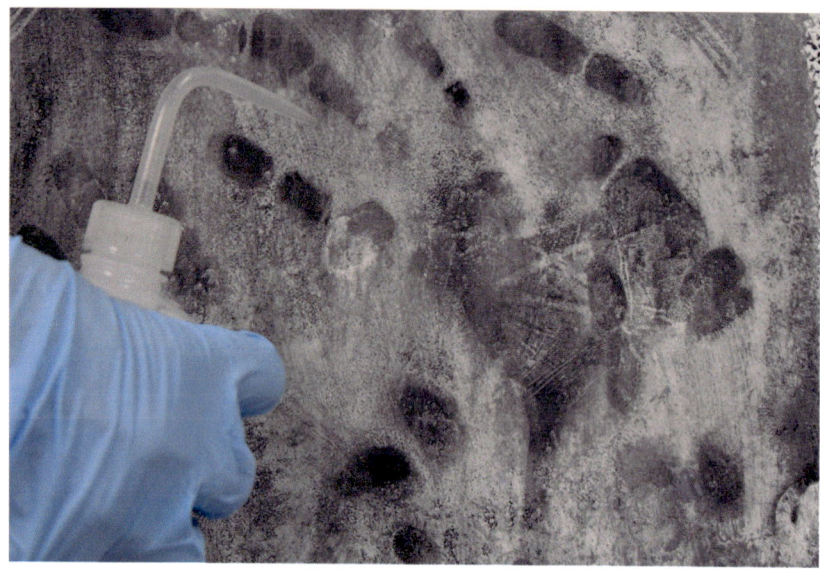

Figure 5.61 Rinse Small Particle Reagent on wet object with distilled water.

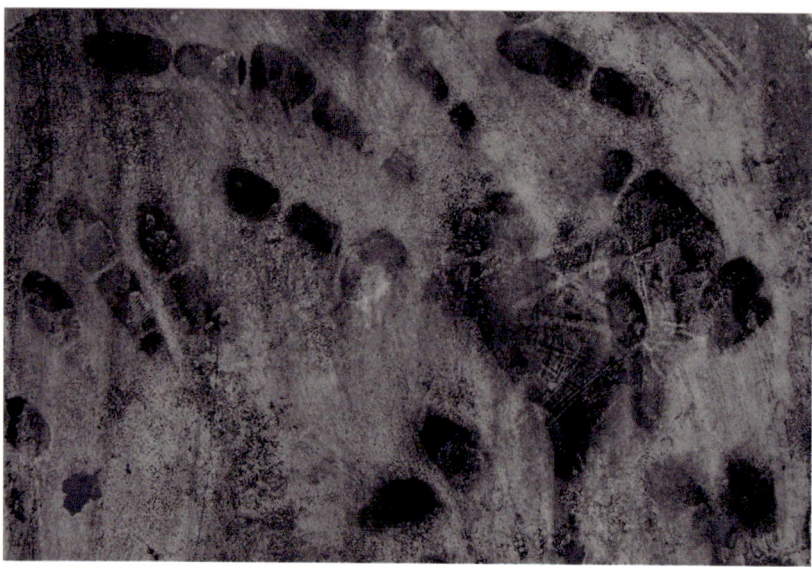

Figure 5.62 Results of Small Particle Reagent; photograph lifts and then lift with latent tape or gel lifter or send the object with results to the lab if possible.

Figure 5.63 Process—step one (after photographs) spray enhancement chemical (Amido Black).

has been bestowed on their ability. There are three possible conclusions an examiner may reach: an identification, a nonidentification, or an inconclusive.

Let us first examine the identification or nonidentification and how those conclusions are arrived at. Through a process coined ACE-V, the fingerprint examiner conducts a comparison. The process allows the examiner the ability to conduct a process whereby all of the information presented to the examiner is ingested and evaluated; then a conclusion is

Figure 5.64 Spraying chemical.

arrived at *m* a hypothesis, if you will. Various levels of information are also incorporated into the comparison process.

> **A**—*Analysis:* Analysis is based on the initial information presented to the examiner. In the analysis, the examiner makes a determination of the quality of the print based on a myriad of factors such as substrate, matrix, development medium, deposition pressure, pressure distortion, and anatomical aspects. *Is the print of sufficient quality and clarity for a comparison and identification (individualization) or elimination?*

Known/Direct/Inked Fingerprints

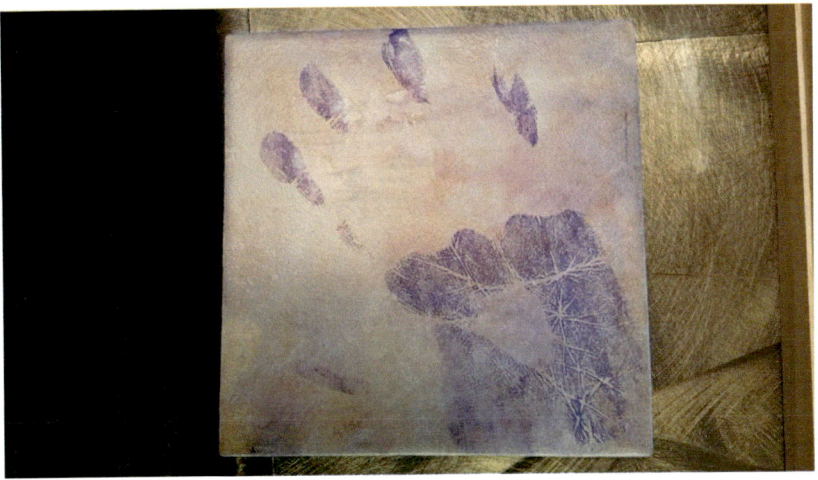

Figure 5.65 Results from enhancement chemical.

C—*Comparison*: What information is contained within the print? Information such as pattern type, friction ridges, flexion creases, major ridge deviations, sequence, and how the two compare to the exemplar print are considered.

E—*Evaluation*: Evaluating all of the information contained in the latent print, specifically the *uniqueness* and *individuality* of the print, the clarity, and the quality. Two questions are asked at this juncture:

1. Is there agreement of the friction skin, flexion path, and configuration?
2. In the opinion of the expert, is there sufficient volume of uniqueness of details in agreement to eliminate all other possible donors?

Note: If the answer is *yes to both questions*, an opinion of individualization and identification has been formed (a positive identification and individualization). If the answer is *no to one or both questions*, an opinion of individualization and identification has *not* been formed (a negative or no identification).

V—*Verification*: All work, as in any science, must be subject to review. This portion of the process employs such peer review. Consultation with another expert to verify the opinion of the original examiner is undertaken at this point. Should there be disagreement regarding the identification, a third person may be used for verification purposes. Just as in any other science, there may be disagreements. Those disagreements must be resolved before an identification can go forward.

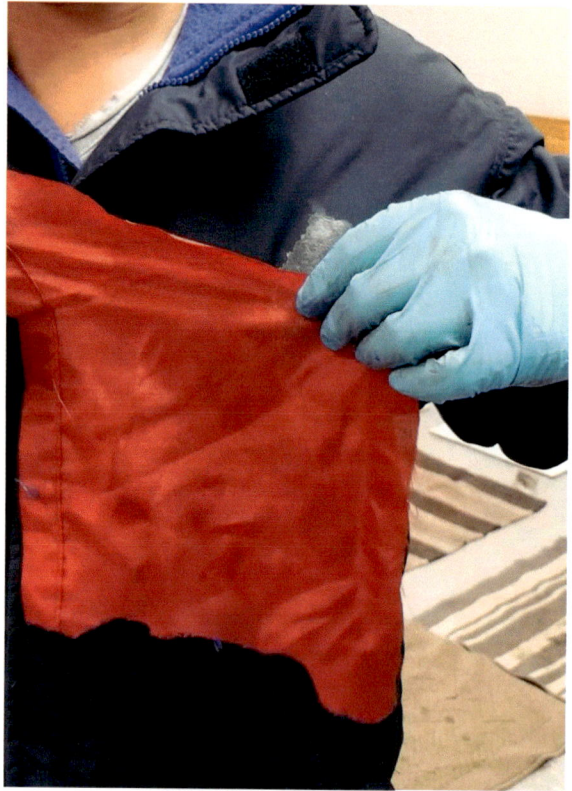

Figure 5.66 Fabric without chemicals.

The examination process is undertaken by various means, including the use of magnifying glasses, comparators, or other means of magnification. The original documents of both the known exemplar and latent are used for purposes of comparison. Copies should not be used to render an identification unless it can be determined that the same high-quality resolution exists between the original and the copy.

As has been alleged in the past, there is a certain numerical requirement needed to affect an identification or individualization. There is no justifiable reason or statistical evidence for a specific numerical requirement to affect identification. Based on the skill and expertise of the examiner, a conclusion will be rendered based on the totality of information presented to the examiner during the comparison process, and not simply a numeric designation. This brings about the question: What if there are differences between the known exemplar and the latent print. *Where an unexplained discrepancy exists, the conclusion should be one of nonidentification.*

There are many reasons a latent and known print may deviate slightly. However, that deviation does not automatically render the print a

Known/Direct/Inked Fingerprints

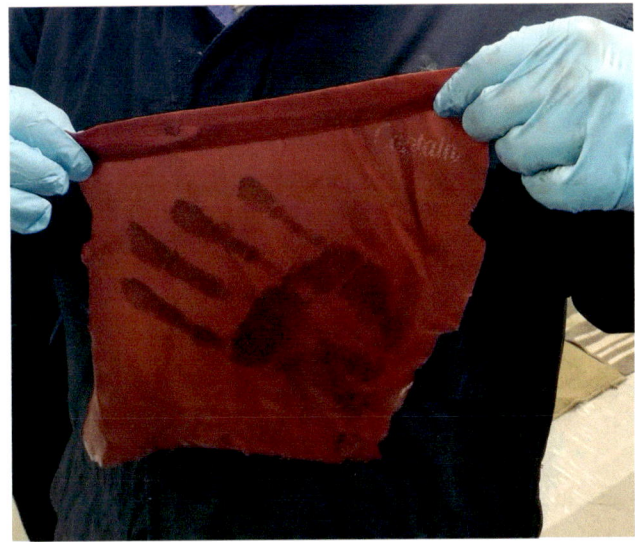

Figure 5.67 Results from enhancement chemical.

Figure 5.68 Area prior to processing with detection chemical.

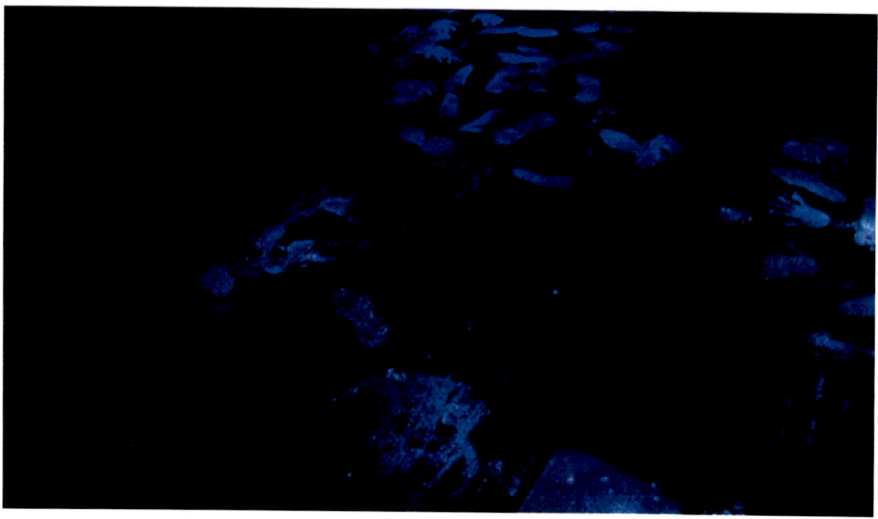

Figure 5.69 Area when processed with Bluestar, detection chemical.

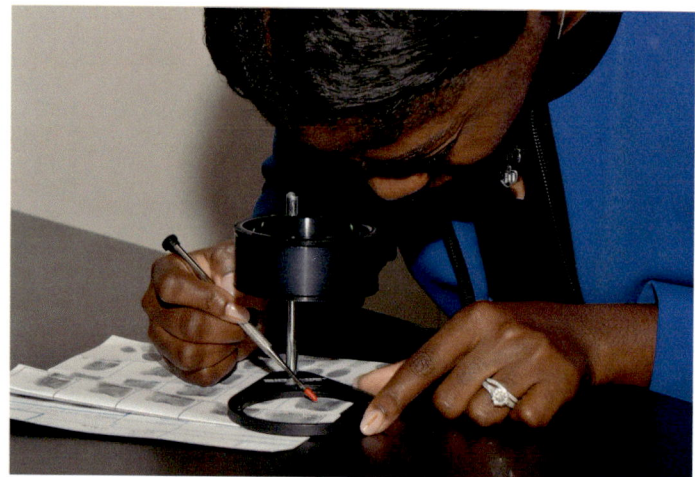

Figure 5.70 Evaluation of fingerprints.

nonidentification. Earlier in this chapter, there were many factors listed that affect the presence of a latent print. Those same factors may become part of the deviation explanation. That a latent print is not good enough to be used for identification purposes does not mean the print may not be used for elimination purposes. For example, a latent print may not possess sufficient ridge characteristic information to conclude an identification/

Known/Direct/Inked Fingerprints 141

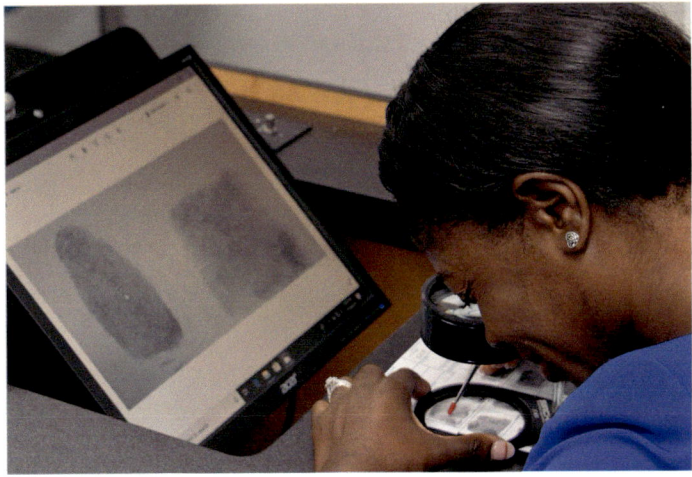

Figure 5.71 The identification process. Example of a fingerprint identification exhibit. The typical exhibit should be clear, concise, and uniform. Although there is no specific number of "points" or ridge characteristics, presenting a uniform exhibit makes the information understandable. After all, it is the trier of fact (judge/jury) who will be analyzing the information during the deliberation.

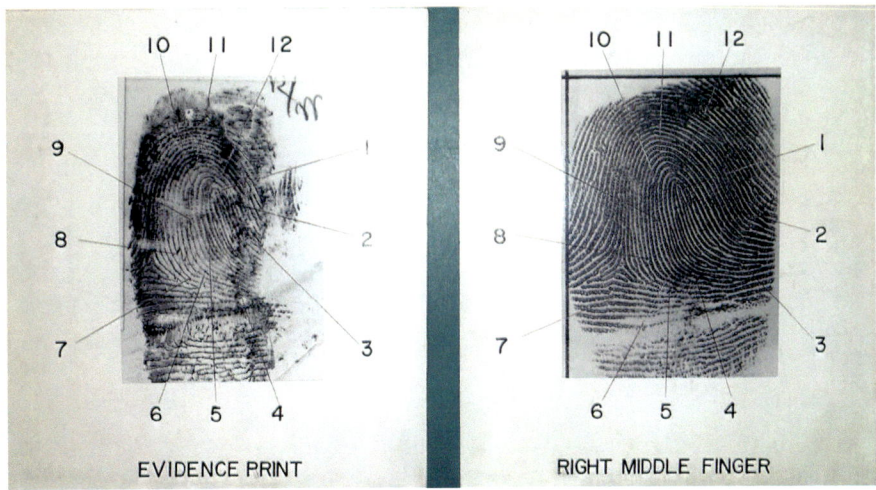

Figure 5.72 Fingerprint identification chart.

individualization, but there may be sufficient information such as pattern type to eliminate a possible subject.

The third type of conclusion that may be reached by the latent print examiner, *inconclusive*, means that the latent print and/or the known print

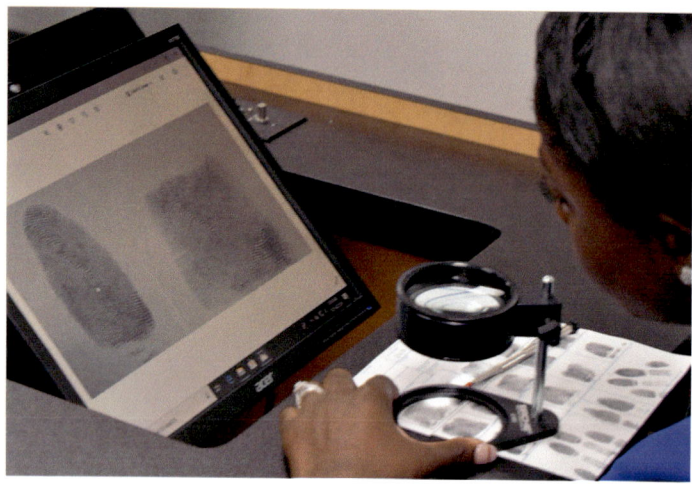

Figure 5.73 Fingerprint evaluation process.

possesses insufficient information for a comparison and/or conclusion. Insufficient information may be due to a variety of factors, as stated earlier in the book.

Additionally, in conjunction with ACE-V for the comparison process, the examiner also takes into account three levels of comparison. The three levels are not used as a replacement for ACE-V but rather as a complement. The levels have simply been termed level 1, level 2, and level 3. What does each level represent?

Level 1: Sufficiency and *clarity* of information confronting the examiner. Is there enough information, pattern type, flow, and ridge characteristics (Galton details) to ensure the quality of the print is a usable print? If the answer to the question is yes, then one can proceed to level 2.

Level 2: Spatial relationship and *type of characteristics* within the pattern are used to determine that the known and the unknown were made by the same individual.

Level 3: Ridgeology and *poroscopy*. At this level, the study of the structure of the ridges and the pores within the ridges is undertaken. Level 3 information in the latent print is often absent due to the quality of the print. The lack of level 3 information does not mean an individualization cannot be made. In fact, identification/individualizations are made even in the absence of level 3 information. More often than not, levels 1 and 2 information is the only information that is present for identification/individualization purposes. Where level 3 information presents itself, the information greatly enhances the individualization perspective. When all of the levels of information have been assessed and the ACE-V process has been undertaken, an appropriate conclusion can be arrived at by the latent print examiner.

Chapter 5 Study Questions

1. Describe the procedure for taking fingerprints.
2. What two types of impressions are placed on the fingerprint card?
3. In which direction are the thumbs and fingers rolled?
4. What are the usual causes of poor impressions?
5. Will excessive perspiration affect the impression? How can we avoid this?
6. What is the procedure followed when the person to be printed has more than ten fingers?
7. How are impressions of crippled or deformed fingers taken if we are unable to roll them?
8. Described the equipment used in taking inked fingerprints manually.
9. What is the most common type of physical evidence?
10. What is a direct/latent/patent/plastic fingerprint impression?
11. What is a latent print composed of?
12. Can we determine the age of a latent impression?
13. Can a person's age or sex be reliably determined from their fingerprint?
14. What are some conditions that may affect the presence of a latent print?
15. What are the primary responsibilities of an officer upon arrival at a crime scene?
16. What is sequential processing?
17. When should a latent print be photographed?
18. What is the order of chemical processing?
19. Define a fingerprint comparison.
20. If there is one unexplained discrepancy between the known and latent print, what finding must the expert conclude?
21. Can two fingerprint examiners disagree on an identification? Explain.
22. What two concerns will always be present when handling evidence?
23. Generally speaking, what is the most important area at a crime scene?

Court Preparation and Presentation

6

Every fingerprint examiner may be called on to testify about the identification or nonidentification of a fingerprint. This process, while sometimes daunting, may be undertaken as a professional through practice and persistence. Like anything else in life, the inexperienced examiner may be intimated initially by the setting of the courtroom and all of the court attaché. As one becomes more experienced and comfortable, the process of presenting a case in court becomes more manageable. As a witness, the fingerprint examiner will be called on to testify as an expert. The judge will grant expert status based on the knowledge, training, and experience of the fingerprint examiner. The following are guidelines that the examiner may practice and use to present a case.

During an investigation/comparison, the fingerprint examiner should always bear in mind that a case may end up in court. Having that in mind, examiners should constantly attend trainings, conferences, and conduct research to prepare themselves for that eventuality. There are three distinct phases of the court process one should consider: *preparation*, *presentation*, and *review*.

Preparation of the Exhibit

In preparing for court, an examiner will need to gather all evidence in the case to present to the prosecutor, the jury (if needed), and to the court in a professional and nonbiased manner. However, the preparation begins through the education and training phase prior to comparing fingerprints for testimony.

As a fingerprint examiner, one must receive basic, modern, and advanced fingerprint training to become a credible witness. For example,

Figure 6.1 Identifying the characteristics within the fingerprint.

having a basic knowledge of fingerprint patterns, knowing the unique characteristics that may be found within a fingerprint, and the ACE-V methodology will be of great advantage during testimony (Figure 6.1). In the long run, having such credentials will also assist the examiner in qualifying as an expert witness.

Another aspect of the preparation phase includes preparing the evidence for the court. A fingerprint examiner should bring the physical evidence, or comparison cards, and results to the court. In cases where an examiner needs to explain the process of comparison to the jury, visual aids may be useful in explaining to the lay witnesses.

Keep in mind that the chain of custody and integrity of the evidence must be maintained. Visual aids may include fingerprint lift cards, comparison enlargements, tenprint cards, and photographs. Be sure that the enlargements and photographs are clear and free from distortion in the ridge details of the fingerprints. Additionally, one may need to generate a brief report that includes the procedures taken to process, analyze, and compare fingerprint evidence. If a report is generated, it must entail important dates, times, and case numbers. Check the report, proofread, and ensure that it is free from any errors prior to presenting in court.

Courtroom Etiquette

Appearance is another key aspect in preparing for court. It is imperative to understand that the role of a fingerprint examiner may determine the conviction or innocence of an individual. Therefore, one must dress in a professional yet unbiassed manner. Consider the following attire while preparing for courtroom testimony:

- Business suit
- Dark color clothing
- Appropriate fit
- Light jewelry
- No sunglasses
- Properly groomed hair

Qualifying the Expert Witness

Another facet to the preparation phase is for the examiner to prepare to testify as an expert witness in the lifting, comparison, and identification of latent and known fingerprints. Although the inexperienced examiner may testify as a lay witness, it will be only a matter of time before the witness is called upon to give expert testimony. Let us first define an expert. By law, an expert is someone who possesses knowledge or skills above or beyond that of a layperson. A more usable or definitive definition would be:

> One who by a combination of knowledge, training, and experience has reached a high level of proficiency in a specific field or endeavor, and who has been so recognized by the court as an expert.

Fewer restrictions are placed on the expert witness. An expert witness may render an opinion while a lay witness may not. The expert witness is also perceived to be of a higher caliber or carrying more weight than lay witnesses.

In order for a fingerprint examiner to qualify as an expert witness, they must undergo the process called *voir dire*, or the questioning of the individual's qualifications. The voir dire is a series of questions that are asked of the witness to establish their credentials as an expertise (see Appendix B). This process can also be referred to as the direct examination of the expert witness. At the end of the examination, the judge will determine if the witness may testify as an expert in the field of fingerprints.

Figure 6.2 Presenting exhibit before the court.

Courtroom Testimony

After the preparation phase, which includes the pre-trial conference or deposition, is completed, the respective parties (defense, prosecutor, and witnesses) should be ready to testify in the courtroom.

The examiner may be called on to testify in a preliminary hearing, before a grand jury, or at trial. One might ask, what is the difference between a preliminary hearing, a grand jury hearing, and a trial? Why should one be concerned about the different types of proceedings? (See Figure 6.2.).

The preliminary hearing and a grand jury hearing are proceedings to establish probable cause to warrant a trial. The extent of the testimony that will be required in a preliminary hearing and before a grand jury may not be as extensive as trial testimony. The examiner who is called on to testify in any of the proceedings must be prepared to testify as an expert and a professional. Personal feelings have no place in the proceeding. *The examiner must remain vigilant, neutral, and testify on the strength of the evidence.* The judge or trier of fact (jury) will make the decision or verdict based on the evidence.

Presentation of the Exhibit

Upon presenting fingerprint evidence in court, whether it be comparison results or actual fingerprint cards, the examiner must always remain neutral. The exhibit should first be admitted into evidence and presented to the judge for approval. The expert witness is then provided the opportunity to introduce the exhibit to the jury for testimonial purposes. When presenting any fingerprint evidence to the jury, it is imperative that the examiner explains in a way for the jury to comprehend. For instance, it is not typical for individuals on the jury stand to understand the daily duties or processes of a fingerprint examiner. Therefore, fingerprint terms should be explained at a basic level of understanding (Figure 6.3).

The historic case that allowed fingerprint evidence in the courtroom (*People v. Jennings*, 1911)

This case would be the first court case that allowed fingerprint evidence into the courtroom. The fingerprints that were presented in *People v. Jennings* positively identified Thomas Jennings as the killer of Clarence Hiller.

> On September 10, 1910, Thomas Jennings burglarized Mr. Hiller's residence and made contact, they were involved in a physical altercation causing them to fall down the stairs. Mr. Hiller was shot twice by Thomas Jennings and fled the scene when Mrs. Hiller screamed out. Mr. Hiller succumbed to his injuries. The residence was later processed, and fingerprints were found in an area that was freshly painted. Later that night Thomas Jennings was stopped and questioned, he was also found to be carrying a loaded firearm. Routine records check revealed that he was recently released from serving a sentence for burglary and was on parole. Fingerprints examiners compared the fingerprints from the scene of the murder to fingerprints that were on file for Thomas Jennings, and they made a positive identification. Jennings was later convicted for the murder of Mr. Hiller on February 1, 1911.

Review

As stated earlier, every time you testify, it should be viewed as an opportunity to improve your skills as a witness. The review facet allows for just such an opportunity.

When one completes their testimony, one should confer with other, more experienced, members of the discipline and discuss strategies.

Figure 6.3 Introducing the exhibit to the jury.

Compare notes between what you did and what the more experienced examiner/witness has done. If possible, request a copy of the transcript for review and to share with other members of the discipline. Where possible, a member of your unit, a peer or supervisor, should also be present in court during the proceeding to conduct an evaluation of the examiner/witness testimony and court presentation. Questions you should ask are as follows: What can I do to better present testimony in the future? Were the court exhibits properly presented and understandable? Was my appearance appropriate and professional? Did I use appropriate and understandable language? What is it that I do not want to do in the future? The review phase of the court process is very valuable as an educational tool. But remember, we are our own worst critics. Do not be unreasonably hard on yourself. Do not be unreasonably critical. Do not analyze the "what if's." You can "what if" yourself to death, figuratively speaking. Do not assume a defeatist attitude. After all, we are all human and we make mistakes. We want to minimize any mistakes to lessen the negative impact on a case.

Ultimately, if one assumes a professional posture and practices accordingly, one will not experience the shortcomings of an unprofessional, unprepared examiner/witness. Practice is the key to success. If examiners keep that thought in mind, their future will be positive. To accelerate the learning curve of testifying in court, there are many courtroom testimony courses available. The examiner/witness should, as early as possible, enroll in a courtroom testimony course. How better to become proficient than by practice and training? To borrow an adage from a colleague who appropriately describes the feeling of testifying, "There's nothing wrong with having butterflies in your stomach as long as they are flying in formation."

Challenges to the Science of Fingerprints

Legal issues challenging fingerprints as evidence have long been present within the criminal justice system. Most of the previous challenges have centered on two main issues: How were prints obtained? Have the prints been properly maintained? The age-old issues have been discussed earlier in the book as *legal* and *scientific* issues. These issues have been effectively dealt with by demonstrating that the evidence was obtained in accordance with accepted standards that are common practice within the forensic science community and that the chain of evidence has been maintained. After more than three-quarters of a century of using fingerprints as a form of evidence, the issue of fingerprints and the methodology associated with fingerprint identification has been challenged in recent years, specifically the methodology through which an identification/individualization is made. The challenge to this process has become known as the *Daubert challenges*. Of all the *Daubert* challenges that have been filed (in excess of thirty), none to date has been successful. That is not to say that the field of fingerprint identification is perfect. Challenges only serve to demonstrate that the integrity of the science of fingerprints remains intact and the necessity for the fingerprint practitioner to be trained, proficient, and remain vigilant is critical.

To do a complete analysis of the issues and court cases surrounding the *Daubert* issues in this publication is impractical. However, a quick overview to expose the beginning practitioner to the legal issues associated with *Daubert* is certainly in order, and will provide the practitioner with a foundation and exposure to the some of the legal issues associated with the science of fingerprints.

From a historical perspective, the first case to challenge the issues of methodology and testimony allowable by an "expert" was *Daubert v. Merrill Dow Pharmaceuticals, Inc.*, 509 U.S. 579 (1993). This initial case required the court to decide the admissibility of scientific expert testimony. What was established in *Daubert* was the standard of acceptability of testimony regarding Federal Rule of Evidence 702, specifically five issues:

1. Whether the theory or technique can be and has been tested.
2. Whether the theory or technique has been subjected to peer review and publication.
3. The known or potential rate of error of a particular scientific technique.
4. The degree to which the technique or theory has been generally accepted in the scientific community.
5. The existence and maintenance of standards controlling its operation.

In a companion case, *Kumho Tire Company, Ltd., et al. v. Patrick Carmichael, etc., et al.* (March 23, 1999), the court held, "setting forth the trial judge's general 'gatekeeping' obligation ... applies not only to testimony based on 'scientific' knowledge, but also to testimony based on 'technical' and 'other specialized' knowledge." Hence, the court upheld its posture of allowing expert testimony by other than scientific experts as mandated in Rule 702.

Federal Rules of Evidence Rule 702

If scientific, technical, or other specialized knowledge will assist the trier of fact to understand the evidence or to determine a fact in issue, a witness qualified as an expert by knowledge, skill, experience, training, or education may testify thereto in the form of an opinion or otherwise.

So in a post *Daubert* and *Kumho* era, the application of testimony of experts has been slightly modified. In part, the new application is as follows: If scientific, technical, or other specialized knowledge will assist the trier of fact in issue, a witness qualified as an expert by knowledge, skill, experience, training, or education, may testify thereto in the form of an opinion or otherwise, provided that (1) *the testimony is based on sufficient facts or data*, (2) *the testimony is the product of reliable principles and methods*, and (3) *the witness has applied the principles and methods reliably to the facts of the case.*

The applicability of the *Daubert* standard specifically with regard to fingerprints was established in 1999 in *U.S. v. Byron Mitchell*.

Court Preparation and Presentation

Chapter 6 Study Questions

1. What is the purpose of a preliminary hearing or grand jury hearing?
2. Define an expert witness.
3. Who grants the witness expert status to testify?
4. What is *voir dire*?
5. What are the phases involved in the court process?
6. One cannot communicate. What does that statement mean?
7. Whose responsibility is it to prepare a court exhibit?
8. What equipment and materials are necessary to prepare a fingerprint chart?
9. How many points of identification are necessary to make a fingerprint chart?
10. Why should technical language or jargon be avoided when testifying?
11. Why do witnesses need to be aware of their nonverbal communication?
12. Where a question cannot be answered with a yes or no answer, what should the witness do?
13. Why should the use of adaptors or regulators be avoided?
14. Explain how to present an exhibit in court.
15. _____ is the key to success.
16. Every time one testifies, one should perceive it as an opportunity to do what?

Appendix A: Techniques/Developers

Technique	Reaction	Surfaces/Substrate/Usage
Tests for Fingerprints		
Physical powder dusting	Adherence to oils and water residues of print	Smooth, nonporous surfaces; metals, glass, plastic, tiles, and finished woods
Magnetic brush powder		Porous surfaces such as woods, skin, paper
Oblique lighting and photography	Natural residues of fingerprints	Smooth and nonreflective surfaces
Laser/ALS	Luminescent material in fingerprint residue	Smooth, nonporous, or slightly porous surfaces
X-ray	Adherence of lead powder to fingerprint residues	Smooth, nonporous, and slightly porous surfaces such as human skin
Vacuum coating	Adherence of gold, silver, or cadmium to fingerprint residues	Smooth surfaces such as plastic films, polyethylene, and paper
Chemical iodine fuming	Chemical interaction of iodine with fatty acids and lipid in residue	Smooth surfaces such as paper and human skin
Ninhydrin/DFO (1,8-diazafluoren-9-one)/physical developer	Chemical interaction with amino acids, peptides, and proteins of residues	Paper, cardboard, unfinished wood
Super Glue (cyanoacrylate ester)	Chemical reaction with amino acids and water molecules	Plastic, metal, glass, cloth
Gentian violet Sticky Side Powder	Chemical reaction	Tapes, adhesive surfaces

(*Continued*)

Technique	Reaction	Surfaces/Substrate/Usage
Small Particle Reagent (SPR)	Physically adheres to lipids and fats	Sticky surfaces, wet surfaces
Ardrox Dye Stain—Alcoholic premix	It provides excellent ridge detail when the latent print is saturated with Ardrox. Prints fluoresce yellow/green when viewed under a light source (Evident)	This fluorescent spray is designed for enhancing latent prints that have been developed with cyanoacrylate
Basic Yellow 40 Dye Stain	Prints fluoresce bright yellow/green between 365 nm and 485 nm with a forensic light source or a UV light (Evident)	Basic Yellow 40 Dye Stain is designed to enhance latent fingerprints developed with cyanoacrylate on non-fluorescent, multi-colored surfaces
Crystal Violet, (Gentian Violet)	Crystal Violet may be applied by either dipping or brushing the solution onto the adhesive side of tape (Evident)	Commonly used for developing latent prints on the adhesive side of virtually all types of tape
1,2-Indanedione Reagent	1,2-Indanedione Reagent reacts with the amino acids in fingerprint residues and produces fluorescent products that render latent prints visible (Medtech Forensics)	1,2-Indanedione Reagent is a chemical alternative for DFO in chemical processing for latent prints on porous surfaces and is generally utilized prior to processing with ninhydrin
MBD	MBD is a dye stain consisting of MBD dye, 4-(4-methoxybenzylamino)-7-nitrobenzofuran, in a mixture of organic solvents	MBD has been noted to be an excellent dye for cyanoacrylate-developed prints on nonporous objects
Nile Red Dye Stain	Nile Red is fluorescent when exposed to a forensic light source between 450 nm and 560 nm, making it ideal for use with a wide variety of forensic light sources (Evident)	Nile Red Dye Stain is often used after cyanoacrylate processing on multi-color surfaces

(Continued)

Appendix A

Technique	Reaction	Surfaces/Substrate/Usage
Oil Red O (ORO)	Oil Red O (ORO) is a lipid stain which is used for enhancing latents produced by the lipids commonly found in foodstuffs, oils, cosmetics, and other fatty substances	Oil Red O has been found to be particularly useful in revealing latents on porous surfaces that have been wet, a process that normally removes the amino acids, salts, etc., which are the basis of conventional chemical processing methods
R.A.M. Dye Stain—Rhodamine, Ardox, and MBD	R.A.M. Dye Stain is a fluorescent stain mixture of Rhodamine 6G, Ardrox, and MBD. Use R.A.M. with a forensic light source after processing with cyanoacrylate	Particularly useful in the enhancement of cyanoacrylate developed prints on plastic bags. R.A.M. enhanced latent prints are visualized between 415 nm and 530 nm, making it ideal for use with a wide variety of forensic light sources. Provided as a 32 oz. premix bottle or concentrate. Mix concentrate with 1 L of solvent (Evident)
Rhodamine	Rhodamine Premix is a dye consisting of Rhodamine 6G dye in a mixture of organic solvents	Rhodamine has been noted to be an excellent dye for cyanoacrylate developed prints. Longwave UV, Laser, or ALS is a suitable light source in order to visualized dyed prints (Medtech Forensics)
Leucocrystal Violet	Leucocrystal Violet is commonly used to enhance bloodstained fingerprints and footwear impressions	Leucocrystal Violet will not enhance a print composed solely of normal latent print residues, so it is used only in cases with blood-contaminated impressions. LCV is nearly colorless when first mixed, but is

(Continued)

Technique	Reaction	Surfaces/Substrate/Usage
		oxidized by the catalytic action of hemoglobin in the bloodstain, and will convert to a blue-colored solution, which will then stain the bloodstain
Sudan Black	Sudan Black is a dye that stains the fatty components of sebaceous sweat to produce a blue-black image	Particularly useful on surfaces contaminated with grease, food residue, or dried soft drink deposits. It is also quite useful as a dye stain for cyanoacrylate developed prints. Sudan Black may be used on nonporous surfaces such as glass, metal, and plastics particularly if these surfaces are contaminated with greasy or oily materials

Tests for Blood Detection

Technique	Reaction	Surfaces/Substrate/Usage
Blue Star	Bluestar Forensic Blood Reagent is a blood enhancement reagent whose purpose is to reveal bloodstains that have been washed out, wiped off, or are invisible to the naked eye	Based on its chemiluminescence, the unique formula qualifies it as the most effective blood reagent
Fluorescein	Fluorescein causes a catalytic reaction to occur between the hemoglobin in blood and oxygen. This reaction produces a luminescent stain that will luminesce in the dark when excited with UV or ALS	This product is commonly used to detect blood spatter, bloodstained fingerprints, and footwear impressions, as well as, blood evidence which has been concealed or cleaned (Evident)

Appendix B

It is a well-established fact that the best way to present a case is to properly prepare the case before going to court. The preparation phase of the case means conducting pretrial conferences for both preliminary procedures as well as for the trial itself. This material refers to issues, questions, and the type of questions that should be asked during direct examination of the "expert witness."

Protocol for Preliminary Examination

Preparation

1. Look at and evaluate what type of evidence is at issue.
2. Who are the investigators involved in this case?
3. What is the extent of their experience and training?
4. Was the property merely booked into police property, or was that property processed for the presence of latents?
5. Were latent fingerprints developed?
6. Were photographs taken?
7. Photos by photo lab or crime scene investigation or field personnel?
8. Were the latent prints compared based on a request, or were the latent prints identified with the aid of AFIS (Automated Fingerprint Identification System)? Ask the investigator to explain.
9. If an identification was effected, are there any prints that remain unidentified?

Expert Fingerprint Testimony—Preliminary Examination

A preliminary hearing examination will be less vigorous than a trial examination. However, the qualifications of the expert witness must be established just as in a trial. Proper *voir dire* is essential to getting pertinent evidence introduced. The following questions may assist the district attorney in both the preliminary and the trial examinations (the first set of items, 1 through 31, will often be used for preliminaries).

1. State your name.
2. What is your occupation or profession?
3. By whom are you employed?
4. What is your current assignment?
5. How long have you been working in this capacity?
6. Have you received any special training in the developing, lifting, and comparison of latent fingerprints? Do you possess any special certificates or degrees?
7. At this point, the assistant district attorney may want to ask the defendant's attorney for a stipulation regarding the witness's expertise. (It is recommended that for a jury trial, the witness recites their qualifications and not stipulate.) If stipulation, skip to question 16. If no stipulation, continue on to question 8.
8. What was that training and experience?
9. Are you a member of any professional associations concerned with the science of fingerprints?
10. Have you ever held any positions, offices, or appointments in any of these professional organizations?
11. Have you ever taught fingerprint science in any accredited agencies or institutions?
12. Have you ever presented or published any papers or articles dealing with the science of fingerprinting?
13. Have you ever testified previously to fingerprint identifications?
14. On how many occasions and at what levels of court (municipal/state/federal)?
15. Ask the court to certify the witness as an expert witness if there are no objections.
16. What is a latent print?
17. On _____, did you go to _____?
18. What was the reason you went to _____?
19. Did your investigation reveal any latent prints?
20. Where did you locate the prints (what room and item)?
21. After locating and developing the latent prints, what did you do with them?
22. Did you bring those latent prints with you today?
23. Have all fingerprint cards (lifts) and envelopes marked?
24. Did you compare the latent prints from _____ marked _____ with any known prints?
25. At this time you may want to ask, "What is a known or inked print?"

Appendix B

26. Are you the custodian of record of the known prints?
27. Did you bring those known prints with you to court today? (Ask for a stipulation that the known prints are those of the defendant. If not, lay a foundation as a business record.)
28. Have the known prints been marked?
29. What was the result of your examination and comparison? (What was your conclusion?)
30. Thank you. Nothing further.
31. After cross and redirect (if needed), have latent and known prints of the defendant entered into evidence?

Expert Fingerprint Testimony—Jury Trial

In addition to your experience, education, certifications, and affiliations, the following questions relative to the field of identification could be asked. The qualified examiner should be able to answer the questions.

1. What conclusions may be arrived at by the examiner?
2. What is a latent impression?
3. What is an inked or known impression?
4. How is an identification effected (basic premise)?
5. Is there a specific number of "points" that one must find to conclude a positive identification?
6. What is meant by dissimilarities?
7. What do you mean by an apparent explainable dissimilarity?
8. What is a natural dissimilarity?
9. How many points of dissimilarities must you find in order to exclude a person?
10. When conducting a comparison, at what point in time do you conclude an identification or eliminate a person?
11. What is the basic premise of fingerprint identification?
12. Can two examiners differ in an opinion?
13. Is fingerprint identification an exact science?
14. If yes, then why would two examiners differ in their opinion?
15. Could you determine exactly the age of the latent impression (technically or generally)?
16. How many points of identification are contained in a normal rolled ink or live scan impression?
17. Did you examine the dissimilarities that are present (that is, microscopically)?
18. If you were to find ten points of identification and one dissimilarity, would you exclude the identification?

19. How many points have you found similar to someone else's?
20. What is a lift card?
21. What is lifting tape?
22. What are the methods employed in the development of latents and how do those methods work (powders/chemicals)?
23. What books or publications have you read regarding the science of fingerprints?
24. Can fingerprints be forged?
25. Can you tell in all instances that a print has been forged?
26. What is a transferred fingerprint?
27. How long will a latent print last?
28. What is meant by a reversed print?
29. What is meant by a print of no value?
30. Explain the dusting and lifting process.
31. Define sebaceous oils.
32. What is the makeup of perspiration?
33. Could you eliminate a person even though a latent impression would be of no identification value?
34. Have you ever made an erroneous fingerprint identification?
35. Describe fingerprint minutiae.
36. How many layers of skin are there?
37. What is the average thickness of skin?
38. What is poroscopy?
39. Could another expert disagree with your identification?
40. What is the lowest number of points needed to conclude a positive identification?
41. What do you mean by a sufficient number of points?
42. Is the absence of characteristics just as important as the presence of characteristics?
43. Is it not true every time you see a dissimilarity you guess what caused it?
44. Can a person touch something and not leave a fingerprint?
45. If you cannot lift a latent print, how do you preserve it?
46. What is live scan?
47. What is AFIS?
48. What is IAFIS?
49. What is the process referred to as ACE-V?

Appendix C

Fingerprint Examination Report

02/1/2021

(continued on next page)

Date:	02/1/2021
To:	John Joe, AUSA United States Attorney's Office
From:	Fingerprint Analyst 1: Bracey-Ann Francis
Subject:	Fingerprint Examination Report

To: John Joe, AUSA
United States Attorney's Office

Title: Fingerprint Analyst 1, Fingerprint/Identification Unit
Case ID Number: 20-00000

Examiner: Bracey-Ann Francis
01/15/2021 – Request received from Assistant United States Attorney John Joe, Miami, Florida.

As per our conversation, and per your request, the exhibits examined were as follows:

Exhibit 1 – It is a certified copy of a prior conviction containing fingerprints, labeled as: Fingerprints of Defendant, received from Assistant United States Attorney John Joe, bearing the name of the defendant Jane Doe in case number 20-00000, and other descriptive information.

Exhibit 2 – It is a certified copy of the Arrest and Booking Report containing what is labeled as Right Thumb Print, at the bottom right corner of the report, as well as a certified copy of a prior conviction containing fingerprints labeled as Fingerprints of Defendant, received from Assistant United States Attorney John Joe, bearing the name Jane Doe in case number 20-00000.

Exhibit 3 – It is a certified copy of a prior conviction containing fingerprints labeled as Fingerprints of Defendant, received from Assistant United States Attorney John Joe, bearing the name Jane Doe in case number 20-00000.

Exhibit 4 – It is a standard fingerprint card containing (10) rolled inked fingerprints and a set of plain inked fingerprint impressions, simultaneously taken at the bottom of the fingerprint card, which I collected from the defendant Jane Doe, at the United States Courthouse on January 2, 2020, at approximately 2:30 p.m.

The two fundamental principles of friction ridge identification are uniqueness and persistence, meaning each area of friction ridge skin is unique to one individual, and remains unchanged throughout that individual's life barring any scars or intentional mutilation.

A known/inked print is the deliberate reproduction of the friction ridges located on the joints of the fingers, the palms, and the soles of the feet. Fingerprint impressions are obtained by rolling each finger in ink and placing it onto a contrasting background/fingerprint card.

My conclusions were reached using the Analysis, Comparison, and Evaluation – Verification (ACE-V) Methodology. The following is a description of the method used.

The Analysis Phase is performed to make the observation of the individual impressions. This includes the general flow of ridges; clarity of the ridges and unique characteristics present; and any distortion appearing within the impression. The examiner then determines if the impressions in question contain sufficient information to continue to the comparison phase.

The Comparison Phase begins when two or more impressions have been found suitable for comparison. The impressions are compared using a 3½ inch magnifying glass by following the ridges in sequence to determine if the same ridge detail and characteristics are present and in the same relative space of location.

The Evaluation Phase is when an identification, exclusion, or inconclusive determination is made by the examiner.

In the Verification Phase, a second examiner conducts an independent examination following the ACE methodology described above, providing a quality assurance measure.

Examination Notes: On January 20, 2020, I examined three exhibits, which have since been marked Exhibit 1, Exhibit 2, and Exhibit 3, containing known inked impressions.

Appendix C

Exhibits 1 through 3 contain rolled fingerprint impressions, as well as a certified Arrest and Booking Report containing what is labeled as a Right Thumb Print at the bottom of the report in Exhibit 2. I used the plain impressions on Exhibit 4 to confirm the sequence of the rolled impressions in Exhibits 1 through 3.

The *right thumb* fingerprint impression(s) on all exhibits reveal whorl patterns: with similar size, shape, and flow of ridges, displaying the same minute ridge characteristics and detail in the same space of location. When analyzing the right thumb, specifically on Exhibit 2, directly in front of the left delta, located in the center of the typlines, which is a point of divergence that surrounds or tends to surround the pattern area of the fingerprint, I found an enclosure, immediately followed by a bifurcation. After the bifurcation, there are two continuing ridges leading to the core area of the fingerprint. It was consistent with the #1 finger (right thumb) on the standard fingerprint card, Exhibit 4, of the rolled impressions of the defendant.

The *right index* fingerprint impression(s) on all exhibits reveal whorl patterns: with similar size, shape, and flow of ridges, displaying the same minute ridge characteristics and detail in the same space of location.

The *right middle* fingerprint impression(s) on all exhibits reveal whorl patterns: with similar size, shape, and flow of ridges, displaying the same minute ridge characteristics and detail in the same space of location. When analyzing the right middle finger, specifically on Exhibit 3, above the core area of the fingerprint pattern, I found a ridge ending. After the ridge ending, there is a bifurcation, which is followed by another ridge that comes to an end in the middle of the pattern area. These findings are consistent with characteristics in the same space of location on finger #3 (right middle) as on the standard fingerprint card Exhibit 4 of the rolled impressions of the defendant.

The *right ring* fingerprint impression(s) on all exhibits reveal whorl patterns: with similar size, shape, and flow of ridges, displaying the same minute ridge characteristics and detail in the same space of location. When analyzing the right ring finger, specifically on Exhibit 1, directly below the core of the whorl pattern, I found a bifurcating ridge. Below that bifurcating ridge are two continuing ridges, which lead towards the center of the two deltas.

The *right little* fingerprint impression(s) on all exhibits reveal loop patterns: with similar size, shape, and flow of ridges, displaying the same minute ridge characteristics and detail in the same space of location.

The *left thumb* fingerprint impression(s) on all exhibits reveal whorl patterns: with similar size, shape, and flow of ridges, displaying the same minute ridge characteristics and detail in the same space of location.

The *left index* fingerprint impression(s) on all exhibits reveal whorl patterns: with similar size, shape, and flow of ridges, displaying the same minute ridge characteristics and detail in the same space of location. When analyzing the left index finger specifically on Exhibit 3, directly in front of the right delta of the whorl pattern, I found a continuing ridge characteristic. In front of the continuing ridge is an enclosure that is followed by a bifurcation. In front of the bifurcation, there is a continuing ridge, which leads to the core area of the fingerprint. The unique characteristics found are consistent with the #7 finger (left index) on the standard fingerprint card Exhibit 4 of the rolled impressions of the defendant.

The *left middle* fingerprint impression(s) on all exhibits reveal whorl patterns: with similar size, shape, and flow of ridges, displaying the same minute ridge characteristics and detail in the same space of location.

The *left ring* fingerprint impression(s) on all exhibits reveal whorl patterns: with similar size, shape, and flow of ridges, displaying the same minute ridge characteristics and detail in the same space of location.

The *left little* fingerprint impression(s) on all exhibits reveal loop patterns: with similar size, shape, and flow of ridges, displaying the same minute ridge characteristics and detail in the same space of location.

Results of the Examinations: The fingerprints presented on the certified prior convictions referenced above as Exhibits 1, 2, and 3 received and marked, respectively, by Assistant United States Attorney John Joe, are the fingerprints of one and the same individual as on the standard fingerprint card marked as Exhibit 4 by Assistant United States Attorney John Joe, which I collected from the defendant (Jane Doe). A second Fingerprint Examiner conducted an independent examination and reached the same conclusion that all fingerprint impressions were made by the same individual.

Bracey-Ann Francis, Fingerprint Analyst 1.

Bibliography

Ashbaugh, D. R., *Quantitative-Qualitative Friction Ridge Analysis.* Boca Raton, FL: CRC Press, 1999.
Collins, C. G., *Fingerprint Science How to Roll, Classify, File and Use Fingerprints.* Belmont, CA: Thomson/Wadsworth, 2001.
Gaensslen, R. E., and Lee, H. C., *Advances in Fingerprint Technology* (2nd ed.). Boca Raton, FL: CRC Press, 1994.
Olsen, R. D., Jr., *Scott's Fingerprint Mechanics.* Springfield, IL: Charles C Thomas, 1978.
U.S. Department of Justice, Federal Bureau of Investigation, *The Science of Fingerprints* (rev. 12/84). Washington, DC: U.S. Government Printing Office.

Glossary

ACE-V – The acronym for a scientific method: Analysis, Comparison, Evaluation, and Verification.

AFIS – The acronym for Automated Fingerprint Information System, a generic term for a fingerprint matching, storage, and retrieval system.

Analysis – The first step of the ACE-V method. The assessment of an impression to determine suitability for comparison.

Anthropometry – It consists of taking specific body measurements metrically and classifying those measurements into small, medium, and large. Body measurements consist of the length of arms, sitting height, caliper measurements of the head.

Arch – A pattern type in which the friction ridges enter on one side of the impression and flow, or tend to flow, out the other side with a rise or wave in the center of the impression.

Arch-Tented – A pattern type that possesses either an angle, an upthrust, or two of the three basic characteristics of the loop.

Bifurcation – The point at which one friction ridge divides into two friction ridges.

Blind Verification – The process of independently examining one or more friction ridge impressions at any stage of (Analysis, Comparison, and Evaluation) by another examiner who is provided with minimal information, and has no knowledge of the conclusion from the original examiner.

Characteristics – The distinctive details of the friction ridges, also known as features.

Comparison – The observation that two impressions have ridge characteristics of similar.

Competency – Possessing and demonstrating the required knowledge, skills, and abilities to successfully perform a specific task.

Conclusion – The result of the evaluation stage of the ACE-V method, including individualization, inconclusive, or exclusion.

Core – The center of the fingerprint pattern.

Delta – The point on a friction ridge at or nearest to the point of divergence of two type lines, and located at or in front of the point of divergence.

Distortion – Discrepancies in the reproduction of friction skin caused by factors such as pressure, movement, force, and contact surface.

Divergence – The spreading apart of two ridges that have been running parallel or nearly parallel.

Evaluation – The third step of the ACE-V method wherein an examiner assesses the value of the details observed during the analysis and the comparison steps and reaches a conclusion.

Exclusion – The determination by an examiner that there are sufficient quality and quantity of detail in disagreement to conclude that two areas of friction ridge impressions did not originate from the same source.

Features – Distinctive details of the friction ridges, also known as characteristics.

Fingerprint – An impression or reproduction left on any material by the friction skin of the fingers.

Friction Ridge – A raised portion of the epidermis on the palmar or plantar skin, consisting of one or more connected ridge units.

Friction Skin – The skin on the inner hands and fingers, and on the bottom of the feet and toes, which is characterized by alternating strips of raised ridges and furrows arranged in a variety of patterns.

Furrow – The portion of the skin lower and between the ridges.

Galton Details – Term referring to friction ridge characteristics, also known as minutiae.

Henry Classification – An alphanumeric system of fingerprint classification named Sir Edward Richard Henry used for filing, searching, and retrieving tenprint records.

Identification – The process of determining that the same finger made two or more fingerprint impressions based on the friction ridge details of both impressions.

Impression – Friction ridge detail deposited on a surface.

Inconclusive – The determination by an examiner that there is neither sufficient agreement to individualize, nor sufficient disagreement to exclude.

Individualization – The determination by an examiner that there are sufficient quality and quantity detail in agreement to conclude that two friction ridge impressions originated from the same source.

Latent Print – An impression caused by perspiration through the sweat pores on the friction ridges of the skin being transferred to another surface.

Loop – This pattern accounts for 60–65 percent of fingerprint patterns. The loop pattern is the most common. In this pattern type, the ridges enter upon one side, recurve, touch, or pass an imaginary line between the delta and the core and flow out, or tend to flow out on the same side the ridges entered.

Minutiae – Events along a ridge a path, including bifurcations, ending ridges, and dots (also known as Galton Details).

Glossary

NCIC – The acronym stands for the National Crime Information Center, which is a computerized database of wanted persons.

Palm Print – An impression of the friction ridges of all or any part of the palmar surface of the hand.

Pattern Area – The part of a loop or whorl pattern in which the cores, deltas, and ridges appear, which we are concerned with in classifying.

Pattern Type – The fundamental pattern of the ridge flow.

Persistence – Fingerprints are formed during the gestation period in the womb and do not change throughout an individual's lifetime, however, barring any scars or intentional mutilation.

Proficiency – The ongoing demonstration of competency.

Quality – The clarity of information contained within a friction ridge impression.

Quantity – The amount of information contained within a friction ridge impression.

Radial Loop – Loop pattern in which the ridges flow toward the thumb.

Ridge Flow – The direction of one more friction ridges.

Ridge Counting – The number of ridges intervening between the delta and the core.

Sufficient Recurve – The part of a recurving ridge between the shoulders of a loop. It must be free of any appendage abutting upon the outside of the recurve at right angles.

Tenprint – A controlled recording of an individual's available fingers using ink, electronic imaging, or other medium.

Type Lines – The two innermost friction ridges associated with a delta that parallel, diverge, surround, or tent to surround the pattern area.

Ulnar Loop – Loop pattern in which the ridges flow toward the little finger.

Uniqueness – Means there are likely no two people in this world with the same fingerprint, not even identical twins.

Verification – The independent application of the ACE process used by another examiner to support refuting the conclusions of the original examiner, can be conducted as a blind verification.

Whorl—Accidental – A pattern type consisting of the combination of two different types of patterns, with two or more deltas.

Whorl—Central Pocket Loop – The central pocket loop whorl has two deltas and at least one ridge making a complete circuit, which may be spiral, oval, circular, or any variant of a circle.

Whorl—Double Loop – A double loop whorl pattern consists of two separate loop formations with two separate distinct sets of shoulders and two deltas.

Whorl—Plain – A plain whorl possesses two deltas, and at least one ridge making a complete circuit, which may be spiral, oval, circular, or any variant of a circle.

Index

advanced fingerprint training, 145
analogs for fingerprint development techniques, 122
Analysis, Comparison, and Evaluation – Verification (ACE-V): methodology, 146, 164; process, 135–137
anonymity, 12
anthropometry: definition, 16; principles of, 16
arch patterns, 24
ardrox dye stain—alcoholic premix, 120
ardrox dye stain—aqueous premix, 120
artist rendering: challenges, 15; exact likeness of an individual, 15; identification of, 15
Automated Fingerprint Identification System (AFIS), 9, 59, 74, 132, 159
automated fingerprint equipment, 86–87

Battley system, 74
Bertillon, Alphonse, 6, *17*
Bertillonage, 16–20; anthropometry, 16; body measurements for, 18; *portrait parlé*, 17; shortcomings of, 17–19; use of full face and profile photo, 17; values established by, 19–20
bifurcation, 27
blocking the card, 60
Bluestar reagent, 125–127, *140*
Blue Star Test, **158**
body measurements, for Bertillon method, 18

CAE wand method, 109
Caracatch, Peter, 10
cardholder, 80
Charan, Kangali, 10
chemical technique, 104–108

classification line, 69
classification systems, 59–75
classifying fingerprints, 59
Coomassie Blue, 122
conversion chart, 66
conversion of ridge counts, 66
conversion process, 68
core, 25, *26*, 30; rules governing selection, 30
courtroom etiquette, 147
courtroom testimony, 148
court process, 145; courtroom etiquette, 147; courtroom testimony, 148; preparation of the exhibit, 145–146
"crest" of an arch, 39
crime scene management technique, 91–93
criminal identification, 11–13
crystal violet (gentian violet), 121

Daguerreotype, 15
Daubert challenges, 151
Daubert v. Merrill Dow Pharmaceuticals, Inc. 509 U.S. 579 (1993), 152
delta, 25, *26*, 29–30; rules for choosing, 30
DFO(1,8-Diazafluoren-9-one)/PD (Physical Developer), 113, *119*, *121*
digital photography, 16
divergence, 27
DNA profiling, 27

expert fingerprint testimony, 159–161
expert witness, 147, 159

Faulds, Henry, 6
Federal Bureau of Investigation (FBI), 8
Federal Rule of Evidence 702, 152
Ferrier, Sgt. John K., 8
fluorescein, 125–126
fingerprint card, 60, 69, 81; tenprint, *61*

fingerprint development techniques, 93–94; analogs for, 122; CAE wand method, 109; chemical technique, 104–108; fuming or tenting method, 108–112; iodine, 110; ninhydrin method, 112–113, *117–119*; powder technique, 94–104, *95–105*, 121–122, *122*; procedure after developing prints, 127–130; sequential processing, 127; super glue, *115–116*; using ardrox dye stain—alcoholic premix, 120; using ardrox dye stain—aqueous premix, 120; using basic yellow 40 dye stain, 120–121; using Bluestar reagent, 125–127, *140*; using Coomassie Blue, 122; using crystal violet (gentian violet), 121; using DFO (1,8-Diazafluoren-9-one)/PD (Physical Developer), 113, *119*, *121*; using fluorescein, 125–126; using 1,2-indanedione reagent, 113–114; using Leucocrystal Violet, 122, 124; using MBD dye, 114; using Nile Red Dye Stain, 114; using Oil Red O (ORO), 115–116; using R.A.M. Dye Stain, 116; using rhodamine premix, 119; using Sudan Black, 124

fingerprint equipment: automated, *86–87*; cardholder, 80; fingerprint card, 81; impressions, 82, 83; inking plate, 79; manual, 79–88, *80–82*; printer's ink, 80; roller, 81, *81*

fingerprint examination report, 163–166

fingerprint examiner, 145–146

fingerprint lift cards, 146

fingerprints, 3, *24*, *146*; acceptance of, 9–11; angular formation, 27; classification, 24; comparison, 131, 133, 135; core, 25, *26*, 30; in criminal matters, 25, 27; definitions, 20–21; delta, 25, *26*, 29–30; evaluation process, 137–138, *140*, 141–143, *142*; fundamentals, 23–24; history of, 4–9; identification, 11–13, 131–133, 135–138, 140, *141*; identification (individualization), 24; live scan, 87, 88–89; pattern area, 25; patterns, 24–25;

prehistoric carvings of, 3; type lines, 25; unknown, 89–90

fingerprints at crime scene: latent print, 89–90; plastic impression, 90; print development, 91–93; visible/patent print, 90

fluorescein, **158**

footprint/toe print, 21

Forest, Dr. Henry P. De, 8

friction ridge, 21; characteristics, 25; self-induced injuries and, 23

friction skin, 21; alterations to, 23; constancy and uniqueness of, 22; dermal layer, 22; destruction, 22–23; epidermal layer, 21; structure of, 22

full face and profile photo, for Bertillon method, 17

fuming or tenting method, 108–112; cabinet, 111–112; gun, 111; iodine, 110, *117*

furrow, 21

Galton, Sir Francis, 7

Grew, Dr. Nehemiah, 5

Henry, Sir Edward, 7–8, 59; classification, 73; filing system, 71; primary, 71; secondary, 71; system, 62; classification, 59; components of, 59–60; example of, 60

Henry system with the FBI extension, 59, 69; classification of amputated fingers, 70; classification of bandaged and unprintable fingers, 70; classification of scarred patterns, 70

Herschel, Sir William, 6

1,2-indanedione reagent, 113–114

identification of artist rendering, 15

impressions, *82*, *83*; plastic, 90

Index fingers, 60

inking plate, 79

Integrated Automated Fingerprint Identification System (IAFIS), 73

iodine fuming techniques, 110, *117*

Jennings, Thomas, 10–11

Kia Kung-Yen, 5

Kumho Tire Company, Ltd., et al. v. Patrick Carmichael, 152

Index

latent fingerprints, 89–90; conditions affecting, 90–91; limitations of, 90
left index fingerprint impression(s), 165
legal and scientific issues, 151
legal issues challenging fingerprints, 151
Leucocrystal Violet, 122, 124, **157**
"line counts", 71
live scan fingerprints, 87, 88–89
live scan palm prints, 88
loop counts, 67
loop patterns, 24, *26*, *31–34*, 68; definition, 29; direction of flow, 36; issues with, 36; radial and ulnar bones, 35–36, *35–36*; requirements, 29
loop ridge counting: definition, 34; pattern, *34–35*, *37–38*; procedure for, 34

Malpighi, Marcello, 5
manual fingerprints, 79–88, *80–82*; preparation, 83; problems in taking prints, 84–86, 88; recording fingerprints with coroner's spoon, 83–84; taking palm prints, 84; taking the prints, 83
Mayer, J.C.A., 5
morphological determinators, 17
MBD dye, 114

National Crime Information Center Classification System, 72–73; Arches, 72; inquiry, 74; Loops, 72; Whorls, 72
New York State fingerprint bureau, 74
Nile Red Dye Stain, 114, **156**
ninhydrin method, 112–113, *117–119*

occupational wear, 23
Oil Red O (ORO), 115–116

palm print, 21, 55–57; creases, 57; divisions, 56; live scan, 88; taking, 84
Parachique, Gregory, 10
Parke, Captain James, 8
pattern area, fingerprints, 25
photograph, 15
photographic technology, 15
plain arch: definition, 39; patterns, *40–41*
Polaroid instant cameras, 15–16
police artist sketch, 15
portrait parlé, 17; determination of color, 17; general determinators, 17; indelible marks description, 17; morphological determinators, 17

powder technique, 94–104, *95–105*, 121–122, *122*; cyanoacrylate ester, 106–107; fluorescent, 105–106, 108, *109–112*; magnetic, 98, 100–101, *102–104*; using sticky side powder, 121–122, *122–124*
preliminary hearing, 148
process of manual classification: primary, 61; ridge count, 67; ridge trace value of the thumbs, 67; secondary portion, 64; subsecondary division, 65
Purkinje, Johannes (John) Evangelista, 3, 6
printer's ink, 80

R.A.M. Dye Stain, 116
radial, 24
recurving ridge, 36
reference patterns, 71
referencing: definition, 70
Reibel, Joseph, 10
rhodamine premix, 119
ridge counts, 68
right index fingerprint impression(s), 165
right little fingerprint impression(s), 165
right thumb fingerprint impression(s), 165
Rojas, Francisca, 9–10
roller, 81, *81*

secondary, small letter grouping, 64
sequential processing, 127
skin grafts, 23
small letter groups, 64
Small Particle Reagent (SPR), **156**
Sudan Black, 124
sufficient recurve, 29–30, 32, 36
super glue, 115–116

tenprint cards, 79
tented arches, 33; definition, 39; types, 39, *42–43*
tests for fingerprints, 155
Thompson, Gilbert, 6
Troup Committee, 7
Twain, Mark, 6–7
types of proceedings, 148, *148*

ulnar, 24; loops, 60
U.S. Army, 8

visual aids, 146
voir dire, 147, 159
Vucetich, Juan, 7

West Case of Ft. Leavenworth, 19, *19*
whorl patterns, 25; accidental, *49*, 52–53; central pocket loop, 44, *46–47*, 47–50; definition, 41; double loop, *48*, 50, 52; plain, 43–44; ridge counts, 54–55; ridge tracing, 54; tracing illustrations, 55; types, 41
whorl ridge tracings, 66
whorls, 60
whorl trace: symbols, 65; values, 67

yellow 40 dye stain, 120–121